SMOOTHIES

– FLAVOURSOME, FRESH AND FABULOUS!

Published by Grenadine Publishing 2011
Grenadine Publishing is an imprint of Massolit Publishing Ltd.

Smoothies – Flavoursome, Fresh and Fabulous!
© Stevali Production and Eliq Maranik 2011

First edition
ISBN: 978-1-908233-06-6

Product idea, smoothies and styling: Eliq Maranik
Art Director: Eliq Maranik / Stevali Production
Graphic design and illustrations: Alan Maranik and Eliq Maranik / Stevali Production
Original title: Smoothies – förföriska fruktfantasier för alla smaker!
Translated from the Swedish by Katarina Trodden

All photos by Eliq Maranik / Stevali Production, except:
p. 16, 20, 22, 28, 32, 96, 112, 126, 138 – iStockphoto

Printed in Italy by Jeming Srl 2011

Grenadine Publishing
6 Artichoke Mews
Artichoke Place
London se 5 8ts
United Kingdom
www.grenadine.se

ELIQ MARANIK

SMOOTHIES

– FLAVOURSOME, FRESH AND FABULOUS!

CONTENTS

INTRODUCTION

I hope this book will inspire you and make you as fascinated in composing your own smoothies as I am. You will learn what fruits go together, when and how to buy them and how to prepare them before use. The more you know about it, the more fun it gets!

The way food and drink is presented is enormously important to me. Eating should be a feast for all the senses. Since I am passionate about colour and form, I have chosen glasses and made, designed and photographed all these wonderful drinks with that in mind. Feel free to adapt the recipes according to your own taste or to what you happen to have at home at the moment. I hope this book will inspire you to invent new, delicious combinations, and that many of these recipes will become some of your favourites.

This book is a guide to the process of choosing fruit, berries and vegetables, and it also contains some brief facts about them. You will learn about how to prepare and freeze the produce and about useful tools and utensils. The difference between organically grown and regular produce is explained and there are serving and garnishing suggestions as well as other useful information.

The next section includes 100 amazing smoothie recipes divided into four categories: Fruit and Berry Smoothies, Breakfast and Yoghurt Smoothies, Vegetable Smoothies and Dessert Smoothies. The final chapter is dedicated to some less healthy, but oh so delicious, cocktails made from fresh fruit and berries.

These recipes are predominantly made from our most common fruits and vegetables, but lots of other wholesome ingredients can be added. I give some brief suggestions in the chapter on ingredients. For a more substantial smoothie you may, for example, add fibre, nuts, super berries, powdered berries, nourishing oils or protein powder, but if you suffer from any health problems, do ask at your nearest health food shop whether there is anything you should avoid.

Best of luck!

Eliq Maranik

GETTING STARTED

Choose Your Vegetables, Fruits and Berries Carefully!

Making the right shopping decisions is essential when you are making smoothies – you need to learn to find, select, store and use seasonal produce in the proper way.

Most important when it comes to finding the very best fruits and vegetables, however, is to use your eyes, nose and hands, and to look for organically grown products. The freshest produce is found at your local market or farm shop. You can be sure that nothing you buy there has been harvested before it is ripe in order to survive transportation over long distances. Moreover, prices tend to be more affordable that in the high street.

Take your time, and only buy as much as you are likely to consume within the next few days. Do not stockpile fruits and vegetables unless you are planning to freeze them. Storage reduces the quality of all fresh produce.

Look for firm, fragrant fruits with a healthy colour and without soft, blemished or discoloured parts. Picking out your own is better than buying packaged fruit and vegetables, which is harder to assess.

It is also important to store fruits and vegetables in a place where they will keep well. Remember that some fruits and vegetables should not be kept close together. Tests have shown that many fruits and vegetables that are sold in shops contain pesticide residues – choose organically grown produce that is free from additives, pesticides, have softer skins and are superior in flavour. Organically grown produce is a little dearer to buy, but is definitely worth the expense. Compare organically and conventionally grown varieties to discover the difference and your personal favourites. I keep

a log, which is very useful. Unfortunately, the names of mangos, oranges etc. are not always displayed on the shelf. If the name is not shown, ask! If the staff are unable to answer, find out who can, someone ought to know since this is the kind of information that ought to be supplied on delivery.

There are companies that deliver fruits and veg to your door. These will always provide information on the country of origin and name of what you are buying, and sometimes even the name of the grower.

The single most important factor when making smoothies is choosing the right ingredients. Smoothies and juices are no better than the fruits from which you make them. The better the ingredients, the better the end result. Choose fruits and vegetables in season for best result. Fresh fruit has an intense flavour and taste delicious, while fruit that was harvested some time ago, before it was ripe, and then transported over long distances, is often watery and tasteless. Juices and smoothies can be made from virtually any fruits or vegetables as long as they are properly prepared.

Ripe or Unripe?

Choose fruits that are just ripe for best flavour and texture. Unripe fruit is more acidic, harder and lacks that special flavour. Overripe fruit often tastes too sweet, bad even, and the smoothie will become sickly – the flavours become more intense during maceration or juicing. Overripe fruit such as bananas, peaches or mangos will spoil your smoothie. Choose fragrant fruits that feel heavy in comparison to their size – it is usually a sign of ripeness.

Most fruits ripen at room temperature after being harvested. Some become sweeter and juicier with storage, others become juicier but not sweeter. Citrus fruits are one of the few exceptions, they do not continue to ripen after picking, but they can get juicier by being left out in the kitchen.

Wash all Fruits, Berries and Vegetables

Unless you pick the fruit and vegetables in your own garden, you have no idea how they have been treated in storage and who has touched them, not to mention the amount of pesticides that have been used. Most of them, especially imported fruits and vegetables, are sprayed in order to keep longer. This is why it is extremely important that you wash and scrub everything carefully and peel anything that has not been organically grown. Anything present on the surface will otherwise end up inside your body.

Easiest is to wash all hard fruits and vegetables in lukewarm water, using a soft brush that should only be used for this purpose and then be properly cleaned afterwards. Rinse soft fruit in lukewarm or hot water and rub them or use the soft side of a Scotch-Brite kept only for that purpose. Use a small amount of washing-up liquid and a soft sponge to clean citrus fruits and waxed fruits. Remember to always rinse the fruit properly after using detergents.

You can buy special, organic, detergents for cleaning fruit. They remove wax and dirt from the surface, or squeeze half a lemon into the lukewarm water and soak the fruit for 20 seconds before scrubbing. If the wax is hard to remove, you can use washing up liquid first and then continue with the above method. Peel all fruit that has not been organically grown to be on the safe side.

Even fruit with peels that are not eaten – bananas, oranges, mandarins, melons and mangos, for example – should be cleaned properly since pesticides and waxes adhere to your hands and end up in your smoothie when you touch the pulp.

To Peel or Not to Peel?

Most of the vitamins, minerals and enzymes in the fruit are found just underneath or in the peel, which is why it is preferable not to peel the fruit. You do not normally have to peel organically grown produce, but wash all fruits, berries and vegetables properly in warm water before eating. If you are not using organic produce, I recommend that you always peel off the outermost layer of the skin. Always peel bananas, mangos, pineapples, papayas and avocados. Kiwi does not always need to be peeled. You can leave the skin if you are passing it through a juicer, but if you are using a blender, you had better peel it. Leave the peel on unwaxed citrus fruits if you are chopping or zesting it. If you are using a citrus press you should of course not peel the fruit. It is normally best to avoid hard peels and seeds in your smoothies since these tend to make them lumpy.

Removing Pips and Seeds

Remove big stones from nectarines, peaches, plums, apricots, mangos, avocados and other stone fruit. Soft pips and seeds can be passed through a juicer or blender, but I normally remove them since they add flavour and affect the texture. Dark seeds from, for example, water melon or passion fruit may affect the colour, so try and remove them beforehand. Always remove papaya seeds since they will ruin the flavour.

Preparation and Freezing

Prepare all fruits, berries and vegetables before use. Many nutrients, vitamins, minerals and enzymes oxidize soon after you cut the fruit. If you buy a lot of fruit in season, prepare it, pack it in plastic bags and freeze immediately. Even though fresh produce is always best, produce that has been frozen immediately after harvesting is preferable to fruit that is not ripe or has been stored. Strawberries, raspberries and blueberries only keep for a few days, so always prepare and freeze them immediately unless you are using them straight away.

If you make a lot of smoothies, you should bulk buy fruit in season. Always write the date, number of portions and contents on the freezer bags. Prepare the fruit as if you were using it to make a smoothie, pack in batches of one or several types of fruits and berries. Fruit keeps well for 2–3 months in an ordinary freezer, but can be kept longer in temperatures below -18 °C.In shops and storage facilities, the temperature is usually -18 °C or lower, which is colder than your freezer at home. You should preferably use resealable bags that keep the air out. Try and press out as much air as possible before sealing.

The best method for freezing berries is to pour a small amount on the bottom of a small baking tin and then freeze until they are solid. Then transfer to a freezer bag to prevent them from turning into pulp. Juicy fruits can be prepared in the same way.

When you make smoothies, pour the frozen fruit and berries straight into the blender, mix them with the liquid or thaw before use. It is a good idea to thaw frozen berries if you are using a juicer, or they will not yield any juice.

Using a Juicer

You get more out of hard fruits and vegetables if you extract the juices before adding them to the blender. Easiest is to use a juicer. Note that no juice can be extracted from bananas or avocados, they need to be mashed or puréed in the blender.

Using a Blender

Soft fruit such as stone fruits, berries and tropical fruits are perfect for blending into smooth and juicy purées without any of the nutritional value being lost. Harder fruits (e.g. apples and pears), that produce dense, fibrous smoothies, should preferably be juiced before being added to the blender.

Always Clean the Juicer Immediately After Use

Always clean your appliances with the help of a soft brush immediately after use. It will help extend the life of expensive juicers and blenders.

Organically Grown Produce

Organically grown fruits, vegetables and berries are harvested when they are almost ripe. It means that they have lower water content and a better aroma, they taste better and they are juicier and better for you than conventionally grown fruit. On the other hand, they do not keep as well, they are more sensitive and they may have more blemishes and bruises than conventionally grown produce since no preservatives, additives, pesticides or waxes have been added to prolong their life, make them look shiny and keep their shape. Organically grown fruit should be kept in a dark, cool place and consumed as soon as possible. Normally, you do not need to peel organically grown fruits, simply scrub them in lukewarm, running water. Organic vegetables contain more vitamins, minerals, enzymes and other nutrients than conventionally grown produce. They have high vitamin C levels and contain antioxidants – e.g. vitamin E and carotenoids – that protect the cells in our bodies against cardiac and vascular disease.

Ethylene Gas

It may be useful to know that some fruits and vegetables produce ethylene gas, which speeds up the ripening process, partly for the fruit itself, but also for other fruits and vegetables close by. Apples, pears, melons, bananas, peaches, nectarines, plums, apricots and tomatoes contain high levels and should not be kept with other fruits and vegetables since these may become shrivelled, go off or become overripe. Carrots can become bitter, cucumbers become shrivelled and bananas, mangos and avocados ripen too quickly if they are stored too close to other ethylene-producing fruits. But you can also use them to make other fruits ripen faster. Just place them in the same bowl or bag. Examples of vegetables that do not tolerate ethylene gas well include cucumbers, squash, dill, carrots, lettuce, leeks and zucchini. These should be kept separately.

Use Your Creativity

Do not be afraid of composing your own recipes, but remember not to mix too many different types of fruit; mild juices made from apples, pears, carrots and oranges go well with most other fruits and vegetables, but avoid mixing too many strong flavours. If you are using vegetables with a strong or bitter taste, you can always dilute and sweeten them by using the above mentioned juices. You do not normally associate smoothies with vegetables, but they can be used sparingly. Try making smoothies from beetroot, chilli, spinach, celery, sweet pepper or broccoli juice, or simply drink it neat. Experiment with spices, powdered berries or algae, nuts, seeds, protein powder, dried berries or natural fibres. Do not forget the garnish. Use your imagination!

Why Make Your Own Smoothies and Juices?

The answer is simple: it is fun, it is simple, it is good and my body likes it! Last time I went shopping I noticed many different ready-made smoothies and juices, and new ones are constantly added as we grow increasingly aware of what we eat, that vitamins and minerals are important and that our stomachs need natural fibre. And I am not talking about the manufactured fibre you add to your food, but the natural fibre found in fruits, vegetables and grains. Now that all these products are so readily available, why should you make life more difficult by investing in a whole range of appliances that are difficult to clean, carry home heavy bags of fruit and spend time preparing them?

The advantages of making your own juices and mixing smoothies from fresh or thawed fruits, berries and vegetables is that you always know exactly what is in them. You can pick your favourite ingredients and make sure you always buy the freshest and best ingredients available. Moreover, you can easily adapt the proportions and your favourite flavours. The choices are limitless, and it is hard to stop once you have got used to it.

Always try to buy fruit and vegetables that are in season – it is cheaper and they are more nutritious. Seasonal produce can always be frozen and used out of season.

Smoothies and juices are becoming increasingly popular in cafés; it is great to be able to find alternatives to lattes and sweets, but do ask how and where the ingredients were grown, and watch your smoothie being made. Do not hesitate to ask about the contents and when the fruit was prepared when you are buying a ready-made smoothie since flavour, nutritional value and appearance change soon after it is made. Best of all is when you are actually able to watch the fruit being prepared.

Commercial Brands

Today, there are many serious and committed commercial smoothie brands, suitable for those who neither have the time nor the inclination to make their own. These are usually made from 100% fruits without additives, flavour enhancers, colourings, sweeteners or concentrated fruit juices. However, they are pasteurized in order to keep for as long as up to a week and, unfortunately, with the removal of harmful bacteria, much of the original goodness is lost.

These smoothies are without a doubt a perfectly good alternative, but they cannot compete with a freshly made smoothie made from fresh fruit, cut immediately before going into the machine, and drunk straight away. Watch out for smoothies that contain colourings, flavour enhancers, sweeteners, concentrates and other additives. The label should list nothing except fruit.

Serving and Garnishing

It is important to me that whatever I am about to eat or drink appears appetizing to all my senses. That is why I prefer to serve my smoothies in pretty glasses and garnish them with fresh berries, fruits, vegetables, herbs, edible flowers or anything else I can find around the kitchen. There are infinite ways of garnishing and serving a smoothie or fruit juice – it is rather like serving cocktails that are even more famous for their fantastic decorations and amusing decor. Using various types of ice is another way of adding something extra, look for ice trays and bags with unusual shapes, or freeze berries, edible flowers and herbs in ice cubes for an extravagant, surprising touch. I save all the fun cocktail sticks I can find for later use when I am travelling. DIY shops offer many ideas, or involve the whole family and make your own decorations. Each drink should be impossible to resist. Children, who are often hard to convince, will love it and they will discover that smoothies are cool, especially if they are allowed to shop for ingredients and help out making them. Invite children and adult friends to freeze their smoothies in ice-cream moulds with a stick so they can eat them on a hot summer day. But do not keep frozen smoothie ice cream in the freezer for too long as it will lose its flavour and texture.

As you will see from my recipes, I love to vary my smoothies as much as possible by using different types of glass, flavours and garnishes.

TOOLS

All you need to make a smoothie is a sharp knife and an electric blender or an immersion blender and beaker. However, there are a number of other tools and appliances that can help speed up the process and make variation easier.

A BLENDER is essential for making smoothies. If you do not have one, use an immersion blender and beaker, but a real blender is more fun. Simply place all the ingredients in the container, press the button and pour the smoothie into a glass.

When you are choosing your blender, consider motor capacity, speed, volume and if it crushes ice. I recommend one with a glass container since they are more robust, hygienic and do not get scratched and discoloured as easily as a plastic one. Crushing ice is not essential, but it helps.

A JUICER. If you intend to make juice from vegetables and hard fruits, you will need a proper juicer that extracts the juice from everything from hard root vegetables to soft berries. There are two types: centrifugal juicers and masticating juicers. Remember that different machines perform in different ways and extract more or less juice from whatever you feed into them. I recommend you compare brands before making a decision. If pressing juice is what you are after, you had better invest in a masticating juicer (see below).

A CENTRIFUGAL JUICER processes fruits and vegetables and extracts the juice by pushing the pulp through a fine mesh. These appliances are often less expensive, but produce less juice than a masticating juicer. Moreover, some enzymes are killed because the rotating blades become hot during processing. It causes the juice to oxidize, which means that it does not keep as well as juices that have been extracted in

a masticating juicer. Centrifuged juices should preferably be consumed immediately or within 24 hours. It is important that you clean the centrifugal juicer immediately after use since it is hard to remove encrusted pulp. Use the brush provided.

A MASTICATING JUICER masticates the fruits and vegetables and forces the pulp through a fine metal mesh. They are a little more expensive, but more efficient, and they can deal with larger quantities. Masticating juicers come in different price categories, so think carefully before you make up your mind. The nutritional value of the juice extracted is higher and it retains more of the important enzymes compared to juice made in a centrifugal juicer. The juice should be consumed immediately or within 48 hours. The appliance should be cleaned immediately to prevent the pulp from drying and adhering to the different parts of the machine.

A CITRUS JUICE EXTRACTOR is a very useful appliance. There are many different types, both electric and manual. It is the amount of juice you plan to make that determines the type you need. If you are making one or two glasses at a time, an ordinary, manual juice extractor suffices, they are easy to clean and take up little space. They are also relatively inexpensive. If you are planning to make large quantities, it may be worth investing in a more advanced manual or electric extractor. It must be cleaned immediately after use since it is hard to clean once the pulp has dried.

AN IMMERSION BLENDER is an excellent choice for small quantities. It is easy to use and to clean. Do not use it with ice, since the blades are easily damaged. Immersion blenders are intended for mashing food, not for crushing frozen fruits or ice.

TIPS AND ADVICE

Tone Down Flavours

Some fruits and vegetables have a strong flavour. These should be used sparingly and mixed with milder fruits and vegetables. For example, if you use a lot of chilli and ginger, your smoothie will be undrinkable. Use small quantities and combine with milder juices. If you discover that a flavour has spoilt the taste, add some carrot, apple, pear or orange juice.

Flavour Enhancers

If you find the result is too bland you can add a little lemon or lime juice, it brings out the other flavours. Some fruits – melon, mango and banana, for example – can turn out a little too sweet. Simply add a little citrus juice to bring out their fruitiness.

Thinner Smoothies

If your smoothie turns out too thick or more like a purée than a liquid, e.g. if you have used fruits with too little water content, you can dilute it with a little water, milk, buttermilk or juice. Water is the best alternative if you do not want to lose some of the fruity character.

Thicker Smoothies

If your smoothie is too thin you can add a little crème fraîche, quark cheese, Greek yoghurt, banana, avocado or mango. For an even creamier result, use ice cream or cream; or add some tofu, muesli, nuts or other goodies.

Smoother Smoothies

Some fruits and vegetables are very rich in fibre and make the smoothie thick and hard to drink (e.g. pineapple, pear and apple). If that is the case you can juice or purée the fruits before adding them to the smoothie. Extract the juice by pressing it through a fine mesh and return it to the blender with the rest of the ingredients.

Frozen Smoothies

Add plenty of ice for a refreshing summer smoothie or juice. Remember that the ice melts quickly and ruins the taste if the smoothie is too warm to start with, so you could cool the fruit before preparing it to keep the flavours fresh. Remember that it is better to use too much ice than too little. A small amount of ice melts quickly and you end up with a smoothie full of water. Another tip is to cool the smoothie or juice before turning it into a sorbet or frozen smoothie by mixing in the ice.

Serve Immediately

In order to make the most of the vitamins, flavours, colours and texture you must serve all smoothies and juices as soon as possible after preparation. If you want to save it for later, keep in mind that it needs to be kept in a clean, sealed glass container in the fridge. Preferably no longer than 24 hours since the vitamins begin to disappear straight after the fruit is pressed, and smoothies go bad rather quickly. Homemade smoothies change colour and taste fairly quickly, so I recommend you consume it immediately. Always shake the smoothie before you drink it and serve with attractive berries or sliced fruit to please the eye.

FRUITS, BERRIES AND VEGETABLES

APPLES contain plenty of antioxidants and vitamin C. They are a good source of natural fibre, which contributes to lowering cholesterol levels in the blood. Apples should be kept cool, preferably refrigerated, in plastic bags. They do not keep well at room temperature. Apples produce ethylene gas, which speeds up the ripening process. Stock up on local varieties during the autumn, they are the best. Apples can be frozen after they have been cut into wedges and the cores and seeds removed.

APRICOTS resemble plums, but have a yellowish, furry skin. They contain beta-carotene, which is converted to vitamin A. They also contain a lot of fibre, vitamin C and potassium. The fruits can be left out at room temperature for one or a couple of days, but are best kept at 0 °C. Apricots are often imported to Northern Europe from the Mediterranean region in the summer and from South America in the winter.

AVOCADOS are the fruit of the avocado tree and an excellent source of vitamin E. Buy hard, unripe avocados and keep them at room temperature for 3–4 days. The process can be speeded up by placing the avocados in a paper or plastic bag together with an apple, pear or banana. Ripe avocados keep for about three days in a plastic bag in the fridge drawer. An avocado is ripe when the flesh is spongy and yields to light pressure. It keeps well in the fridge at home, but will form dark spots and remain hard if the temperature is too low. Avocados are primarily cultivated in Spain, Mexico and Israel.

BANANAS are usually sold when they are still green and unripe, and they ripen in contact with other fruits that emit ethylene gas, which speeds up the ripening process. Bananas contain high levels of potassium, vitamin B6 and magnesium. Do not store bananas in the fridge or they will turn black. Always keep them at room temperature, preferably in a separate bowl away from other fruits because of the ethylene gas. Bananas can make other fruits ripen faster. They are delicate and quickly turn brown and blemished if squeezed. Bananas are mostly imported from Central America.

BEETROOTS are mild and sweet. To prevent the red from bleeding, boil them without cutting the tops off. Beetroots contain large amounts of potassium, iron and folic acid. The leaves contain the antioxidant beta-carotene. Beetroots are red, yellow or striped on the inside. They are best kept in a plastic bag in the fridge and keep for about 6 months at 4 °C, but only 10 days at room temperature.

BLACKBERRIES contain some potassium and are rich in fibre. You should not pick them until they are fully ripe. They keep for one day at room temperature, but you can freeze them. The berries are delicate, so pick them straight into a plastic bag, remove the air and freeze immediately. Blackberries grow wild in Europe and North America.

BLUEBERRIES are a rich source of antioxidants. If you pick them in the wild, remember to only pick the blue berries and not the black. If you buy them, try to find a batch with berries that are equal in size and not shrivelled. Blueberries keep for a couple of days in the fridge, but are suitable for freezing. American blueberries are a little larger than their European counterpart, but contain lower levels of antioxidants than the ones that are picked in the wild. Another difference is that American berries are not blue inside and that they do not stain your hands.

CARROTS. Carrots arrived in Europe from Central Asia in the 12th century when they were bright red in colour. Carrots contain beta-carotene, a precursor of vitamin A, which causes the orange colour. Remove

MORE INGREDIENTS

Frozen Fruits and Berries

Deep frozen fruits and berries are becoming increasingly common. These days, you can buy most fruits and vegetables from the frozen food department all year; you can even buy mixed fruits ready for the blender. These are excellent substitutes for fresh fruit if they have been frozen immediately after harvesting.

It is a good idea to freeze your own fruit and vegetables in season. You will always have a ready supply for making smoothies and you know exactly what is in your bags. Moreover, fruit is cheaper and better in season. Instructions for how to freeze fruit can be found on page 12.

Dried Fruits and Berries

Many fruits and berries sold in shops are dried. This is an excellent alternative when it is hard to find fresh fruit. Make sure they are all natural and that they contain no added sugar, oil, flavourings, colourings or preservatives. Organically grown fruits without any traces of pesticides are to be preferred. The best produce lists no other ingredients on the label than the fruit. If you are making your smoothies with dried berries or fruit you should soak them before use – the larger the fruits or berries, the longer you need to soak them. Never pour hot or, worse, scalding water over the fruit since it will destroy nutrients. I always recommend that you wash dried fruit before you soak it unless the label states that they have been washed before drying.

Preserved Fruits and Berries

I prefer not to use preserved fruit in my smoothies, but if you are, remember to use fruit that is not preserved in syrup or contains colouring, flavouring or other additives. Best is if it has been preserved in its own juice.

Berry Powders and Super Berries

If you are unable to get hold of these nutritious berries fresh, you can buy powders that you mix into your smoothie. Powders are made from freeze-dried whole berries, including skin and seeds. They are dried gently at 30 °C to preserve vitamins, flavonoids and minerals. Açaí berries, blueberries, pomegranates, raspberries, strawberries, rosehips and cranberries can be purchased in powdered form. Powdered berries keep for up to 18 months, which is very handy. When you are adding fruit powders to a smoothie, remember that the flavours are highly concentrated.

AÇAI is considered to be the most nutritious superberry of them all. American studies have shown that they can destroy leukaemia cells, and it is famous for its high vitamin and antioxidant content.

GOJI has been called a superberry because of the beneficial effect it has on the immune system. In China, it is claimed to prolong life and the berries have been used in Chinese medicine for thousands of years.

INKA is related to physalis and is considered to be the most nutritious berry in the world. It is extremely protein-rich and has a beneficial effect on cholesterol levels. Other super berries are **MULBERRIES** and **BARBERRIES**.

The best thing about these healthy, dried berries, apart from the fact that you can buy them all year round and that they keep forever, is that they are extremely tasty. Super berries are sold dried or in the form of juice.

Base Liquids

You can make a smoothie with almost anything you like, use your imagination and experiment to find your favourites.

Dairy products: milk, buttermilk, yoghurt, quark cheese, crème fraîche, cream, Greek yoghurt and feta cheese are all suitable, just keep in mind that some of these ingredients are rather fatty and calorie-rich, and should therefore not be consumed on a daily basis. Ice cream, frozen yoghurt, sorbet, frozen fruit juices, frozen fruit and berries can all be used to make iced smoothies.

If you are lactose intolerant or just prefer to avoid dairy products, you can replace them with a lactose-free alternative such as soy yoghurt, soy ice cream, oat milk, nut milk, silken tofu, etc. There is a lot to choose from in the shops, but some of these ingredients can easily be made at home. Oat milk and milk made from nuts and seeds are easy to make. Why not try them instead of dairy products next time you make a smoothie?

OAT MILK is made from porridge oats. Vegans should note that vitamin D from sheep's wool is used in some brands.

SOY MILK is made from soy beans, but you can make it at home from soy flour. It is the most protein-rich of all plant milks. You can also buy soy ice cream or soy yoghurt for your smoothie.

RICE MILK is made from brown rice. It is lactose, cholesterol and sugar free and has a low fat content, but it contains more carbohydrates than cow's milk.

NUT MILK is made from soaked and blended beans or nuts such as cashews, hazelnuts or walnuts.

COCONUT MILK comes from coconuts, which is a seed and not a nut. Some people are allergic to coconuts, but it is rare.

Fibres

The body cannot process plant fibres, but they are good for us since they slow down digestion. Vegetables, fruits and wholemeal grain contain a lot of fibre. Extra fibre can be provided by **OAT BRAN, WHEAT**

BRAN and **GROUND LINSEEDS.** These help to balance bodily functions and are all excellent breakfast alternatives. Fibres help keep up energy levels during the day and give you a feeling of satisfaction after a meal.

Nutritious Flavour Enhancers

CARDAMOM contains plenty of antioxidants, it has a calming effect and aids digestion. Cardamom and ginger taken in the morning is said to cure a hangover.

CINNAMON is the bark of a tree that grows on Sri Lanka. Some scientists claim it has beneficial health effects. Cinnamon is used to flavour stews, soups and desserts, but above all for sprinkling on yoghurt and other dairy products.

COCOA POWDER has been much praised in the past few years, and chocolate bars have almost been given health food status. Cocoa has a beneficial effect on blood pressure and is rich in antioxidants.

GINGER is said to have many healing properties. It has long been used in Chinese medicine. It can relieve articular problems, headache and stomach pain as well stimulate metabolism. But more than anything – it is delicious!

LIQUORICE is naturally sweet, which means that no sugar needs to be added. Eating too much liquorice, however, may have negative effects on muscles and blood pressure.

Algae

Algae are an excellent protein source. We can absorb four times as much protein from the blue-green spirulina alga than from meat. Spirulina has been called 'the alga that could put a stop to world famine'. It is so nutritious that NASA give it to their astronauts in space. Other highly nutritious algae include chlorella, arame, wakame and dulse.

Nuts and Seeds

ALMONDS are energy-rich and contain muscle-building nutrients. They contain some monounsaturated fat and a lot of protein and vitamin E. Almond butter is sold in health food shops and can be used in smoothies.

BRAZIL NUTS are a rich source of protein, selenium and zinc. 70 % of the nut is fat, most of which is omega 6; some of the fat is omega 3. Nuts should be white inside; if they are yellow they have started to turn rancid.

HAZEL NUTS contain large amounts of vitamin E, protein and fat. Like all nuts they should be consumed in moderation.

HEMP SEEDS come from the same herb as cannabis, but the seed is entirely free of illegal substances. The hemp seed – which is really a nut – is the fruit of this herb. Only soy beans contain more protein than hemp seeds. They also contain large amounts of polyunsaturated fatty acids.

LINSEEDS are extremely nutritious and contain, for example, iron, phosphorus, potassium, calcium, zinc and magnesium. Linseeds are sold whole or crushed and aid digestion. Like psyllium husks, they form a mucilaginous layer in the gut, which aids peristalsis. Some sources recommend that you limit your intake of crushed linseeds to around 2 tbsp per day.

PECAN NUTS are the stones of a kind of hickory fruit. They contain 72 % fat, 63 % or which is polyunsaturated. They also contain large amounts of antioxidants, especially the brown outer skin of the stone.

PINE NUTS contain a lot of zinc, iron, protein and polyunsaturated fats.

PISTACHIOS are not nuts, but seeds, so they are safe to eat for those allergic to nuts. Red pistachios are coloured, so you should go for the plain variety. Pistachios contain a lot of fat and protein.

PUMPKIN SEEDS contain zinc and many types of antioxidants, high levels of protein and a lot of polyunsaturated fat. It is a nutritious snack with anti-inflammatory properties. Toast or use in salads.

SESAME SEEDS are made up of 50 % fats, nearly all of which are beneficial. They have a protein content of 18 %. Ground sesame seeds are very useful in smoothies.

SUNFLOWER SEEDS are found at the centre of the sunflower. They are rich in vitamin E, omega 6 and monounsaturated fatty acids as well as vitamin B5, which relieves stress symptoms.

WALNUTS are very nutritious, especially for vegetarians, since they contain large amounts of omega 3 fatty acid.

Protein Powders

Examples of protein-rich powders or products are raw rice protein, tempeh, miso, powdered egg white, ground nuts, soy milk and algae. Spirulina contains as much as 65 % protein. Ask at your health food shop.

Cold-pressed Oils

Enrich you smoothies by adding nutritious cold-pressed coconut, linseed or hempseed oil. Ask at your health food shop.

FRUIT & BERRY SMOOTHIES

NECTARINE & RASPBERRY

2 glasses

3 nectarines

200 g raspberries

2 apples

honey or syrup

Wash all the fruit and berries. Peel, quarter and core the apples and pass through a juicer. Cut the nectarines in half and remove the stone. Blend the nectarines, raspberries and water until smooth. Add honey or syrup to taste.

Serve with raspberry skewers.

TIP: Use honeydew melon instead of nectarines for a sweeter, milder version. If you are in a hurry, use a good-quality commercial apple juice brand instead

Acacia honey comes from the nectar of the *Robinia pseudoacacia*, which means 'false acacia'.
Because of the high fruit sugar content, acacia honey is liquid rather than set.

BLACKCURRANT & RASPBERRY

2 glasses

250 g blackcurrants

250 g raspberries

2 apples

Wash the apples and rinse the berries. Peel, quarter and core the apples. Blend until smooth.

Serve with plenty of berries on top.

TIP: For a more liquid smoothie, juice the apples first or pass them through a fine-meshed sieve.

Both raspberries and blackcurrants contain large amounts of vitamin C.
Freeze the berries after harvesting and use them out of season.

WATERMELON, RASPBERRY & MINT

2 glasses

¼ medium-sized watermelon

250 g raspberries

5 mint leaves

Wash all the fruit and berries. Cut the watermelon in half, remove the seeds, scoop out the pulp and place it in a blender. Add raspberries and mint. Blend until smooth.

Serve with water melon slices and raspberries.

TIP: Juice the water melon, raspberries and mint for a smoother texture.

Watermelon pulp is rich in antioxidants, but the seeds contain even more. So do not spit them out – eat them too. Adding them to the smoothie is not recommended, however.

ORANGE & MANGO

2 glasses

1 mango

4 oranges

½ lime

Wash all the fruit. Press the oranges and the lime, and make sure you avoid the seeds since they will add a bitter taste. Use a potato peeler to peel the mango and dice – remember there is a large stone inside. Pour the fresh orange juice and mango into a blender and blend until smooth.

Serve with orange wedges.

TIP: Adding a few strawberries is delicious.

Mango is not only used to make chutney, it is the new peach! Pick a good mango by smelling it and squeezing it gently. Mango contains beta-carotene, just like carrots, which is supposed to give you a quicker tan.

RASPBERRY & PASSION FRUIT

2 glasses

250 g raspberries

3 passion fruits

¼ cantaloupe melon

Wash all the fruits and berries. Cut the melon in half, remove the seeds and peel and put the pulp in a blender. Cut the passion fruits in half, scoop out the pulp and pass through a fine-meshed sieve. Blend all the ingredients until smooth.

TIP: Garnish with a frosted rim. Pour some caster sugar on a plate, run a lemon or lime wedge around the rim of the glass. Dip the glass into the sugar, or replace the sugar with grated chocolate, cocoa, cinnamon or some other suitable herb or spice.

Raspberries are rich in fibre and good for the immune system.
Pick the fresh berries in season. If you are lucky, you may find them wild in the forest.

BLUEBERRY & CINNAMON

2 glasses

2 apples
250 g blueberries
1 pinch of cinnamon
100 ml water
½ lime
honey

Peel, quarter and core the apples
Place in a blender with the blueberries,
cinnamon and water. Press the lime,
and make sure you avoid the seeds
since they will add a bitter taste. Blend
until smooth. Add honey to taste.

TIP: For a more liquid smoothie, juice
the apples (including the peel) first and
omit the water.

Cinnamon is Italian for 'little tubes'. It is the bark of a tree that grows in Sri Lanka, and it was known by the
ancient Egyptians as early as 1500 B.C. The Arabs told many tales to keep the price of cinnamon high. One of
them involved some birds that roost on a top of a steep mountain where no man could reach, and who fed their
young with cinnamon sticks. In order to get to the cinnamon, the Arabs fed the birds pieces of meat that were
so large and heavy that the nests fell to the ground. No wonder that cinnamon was an expensive spice.

MANGO & PASSION FRUIT

2 glasses

2 large mangos

4 passion fruits

200 ml ice water

passion fruit to garnish

Wash all the fruit. Put one passion fruit aside for garnish. Divide the passion fruits, scoop out the pulp and sieve off the seeds (optional). Peel the mango and cut it into chunks – remember there is a large stone in the middle. Blend the passion fruit, mango and water until smooth.
Serve with passion fruit.

TIP: Get rid of the passion fruit seeds by pouring a little water into the fruit and mix the water and pulp until separated. Pass through a fine mesh and use only the liquid.

Passion fruit is in fact a berry, which is said to relieve asthma. It is a climbing plant that can become 15 metres tall. The dark, purple skin of the fresh fruit is smooth. Unfortunately, the name has nothing to do with passion. The dull truth is that it is closely related to the passion flower. The yellow-skinned Maracuja is another member of the passion flower family.

ORANGE, MANGO & POMEGRANATE

2 glasses

4 oranges

1 pomegranate

1 mango

Wash all the fruit. Press the oranges, and make sure you avoid the seeds since they will add a bitter taste. Use a citrus press to extract the pomegranate juice. Peel the mango and dice, and do not forget there is a large stone inside. Blend the fresh orange/pomegranate juice and mango until smooth.

Top with a few pomegranate seeds.

TIP: To make a 'Sunrise' effect, blend orange and mango only. Transfer to a glass and pour pomegranate juice on top.

Separating the pomegranate seeds from the skin is easier if you first roll the pomegranate against a hard surface. Cut it in half and beat the halves with a wooden spoon to loosen the seeds.

PINEAPPLE & LEMON BALM

2 glasses

½ pineapple

6 lemon balm leaves

Wash the pineapple and lemon balm carefully. Cut the pineapple in half, remove the leaves, peel and the hard centre. Dice. Blend the fruit and lemon balm until smooth.

Serve with pieces of pineapple on the side.

TIP: Pass everything through a juicer instead to make a less pulpy smoothie. Experiment by adding chilli or other spices.

Pineapple is an attractive plant that grows to about a metre in height. When the purple flowers ripen they form berries that fuse together to form the pineapple. It has been said to be good for people suffering from cancer or from cardiovascular or intestinal disease. Allegedly, you will smell sweet if you eat a lot of pineapple. So, there are many good reasons for doing so, even though these claims have to be taken with a grain of salt.

AÇAI & STRAWBERRY

2 glasses

350 g strawberries

2 pears

4 tsp açaí powder

Wash the strawberries and pears. Quarter, core and juice the pears. Destalk the strawberries. Blend the juice, strawberries and berry powder until smooth.

TIP: Use a berry powder of your choice to add flavour and goodness to your smoothies.

In order for us to benefit from all the antioxidants, vitamins and minerals present in açaí berries they must either be eaten fresh or frozen immediately after harvesting. Only 10 % of the berry is edible, the stone makes up the remaining 90 %.

APRICOT & ORANGE

2 glasses

3 oranges

½ lime

6 ripe apricots

Wash the fruit. Press the orange and the lime, and make sure you avoid the seeds since they will add a bitter taste. Divide the apricots and remove the stones. Blend all the ingredients until smooth.

TIP: Use dried apricots if you cannot find fresh ones. They need to be soaked for about an hour before using.

Latin for apricot is *Prunus armeniaca*, which means Armenian plum. It was long believed that apricots came from Armenia, now we know they originated in China, where they were cultivated as far back as 4–5,000 years ago. Today, 85 % of all apricots are grown in a part of Turkey that was formerly part of Armenia. Eat it raw, cook it or use it to make jam or liqueur.

GUAVA & BLUEBERRY

2 glasses

1 guava

200 g blueberries

200 g strawberries

1 passion fruit

honey to taste

Wash the fruit and berries. Peel the guava and cut it in half. Remove the seeds and dice. Cut the passion fruit in half, scoop out the pulp and pass it through a fine mesh. Destalk the strawberries. Blend all the ingredients until smooth. Sweeten with honey to taste.

TIP: The guava can be replaced with honeydew melon.

Guavas contain a lot of white, hard, edible seeds.
One guava can contain well over 600 seeds..

MANGO & STRAWBERRY

2 glasses

1 mango
200 g strawberries
200 ml water

Wash the mango and strawberries carefully. Peel the mango and dice, do not forget there is a large stone inside. Destalk the strawberries and blend all the ingredients until smooth.

TIP: You can replace the strawberries with raspberries.

Did you know that strawberries contain more vitamin C than oranges?
Five strawberries are all you need to get your daily allowance of vitamin C.

BANANA & PASSION FRUIT

2 glasses

3 bananas

4 passion fruits

10 green grapes

½ lime

200 ml ice water

Wash the fruit. Peel the bananas, cut the passion fruits in half, scoop out the pulp and sieve off the seeds. Discard the grape seeds, add the lime juice and blend until smooth.

TIP: Note that no liquid can be extracted from bananas; put them straight into the blender. Bananas add sweetness and bulk to tart and watery smoothies, and can be used in most recipes.

There are some fifty different types of banana in the world. Two types of eating banana have been produced through cross-breading – the sweet 'dessert' banana and the more floury plantain, or 'cooking' banana. Plantains are very common in South America, Africa and India where they are used for cooking in much the same ways as potatoes. Dessert bananas include the apple banana, which is small, yellow, and smell faintly of apples, and the rarer red banana.

MANGO & ROSEHIP

2 glasses

2 large mangos

10 rosehips or 2 tsp powdered rosehips

200 ml ice water

Wash all the fruit. Peel the mango and dice, remember there is a large stone inside. Split the rosehips, remove the seeds and stalks, then chop. Blend the rosehips and water until smooth, then add the mango and blend again until smooth.

Serve with mango on the side.

TIP: When rosehips are not in season, use powdered rosehips instead. It can be found in most health food shops.

Any rosehips that are left on the bush will go black in the winter, but they can still be used for food.

BLACKBERRY, APPLE & CINNAMON

2 glasses

3 apples or 200 ml apple juice

200 g blackberries

100 g raspberries

100 ml water

1 pinch cinnamon

Wash all the fruit carefully. Destalk, core and dice the apples and pass them through a juicer or use a good commercial brand. Blend all the ingredients until smooth.

TIP: Add 4 tbsp of vanilla-flavoured quark cheese instead of water for a more substantial smoothie.

Blackberry is a generic name for a collection of hybrids consisting of some 30 species.
Blackberries are notable for their high nutritional contents of dietary fibres, vitamin C, vitamin K and folic acid.

STRAWBERRY & CHILLI

2 glasses

350 g strawberries

1 lime

½ chilli (+2 for garnish)

100 ml ice water

6 ice cubes

syrup to taste

Wash the strawberries, lime and chillies. Destalk the strawberries and make sure that no green or hard bits end up in the blender. Split the chilli, remove the seeds and white membranes, then chop the chilli. Blend all the ingredients until smooth. Add syrup to taste.

TIP: Replace the strawberries with 2 mangos for another delicious combination. Strawberries and mango go well with chilli, or, why not try adding a piece of lemon grass.

The strength of the chilli is not in the seeds, but in the membranes and the base of the stalk. Water is no remedy against the resulting burning sensation since the strength is in the capsaicin, an oil that is not water soluble. Drink a soothing glass of milk instead.

MANDARIN & MANGO

2 glasses

1 mango

4 mandarins

½ lime

200 ml sparkling mineral water

Peel the mango and dice, remember there is a large stone inside. Peel the mandarins and discard the white pith and the peel (or press out the juice). Press the lime and make sure to remove the seeds. Blend the ingredients until smooth. Pour over ice cubes and fill up with sparkling mineral water.

Serve with a straw and mandarin sections.

TIP: For a more traditional smoothie, blend all the ingredients except the sparkling water. Replace it with 100 ml plain water and 100 ml good-quality apple juice.

Mandarin is a generic name for mandarins, clementines, satsumas and tangerines. The name probably derives from the yellow colour associated with the dress worn by Chinese officials, or mandarins.

GRAPEFRUIT & STRAWBERRY

2 glasses

3 blood grapefruits

250 g strawberries

200 ml water

honey

Wash all the fruit and berries. Peel the grapefruit, discard the membranes and peel. Destalk the strawberries, add the rest of the ingredients and blend until smooth.

TIP: If you do not like the bitterness of grapefruit, use oranges or any other citrus fruit instead.

Strawberries are a cross between two types of wild strawberries, and the resulting hybrid was then crossed with a third variety. This successful blend of wild strawberries was called *Fragaria ananassa*, which refers to them being 'fragrant'. Those allergic to ordinary strawberries can usually tolerate white strawberries, which lack the red pigment.

BLUEBERRY & MELON

2 glasses

½ honeydew melon

200 g blueberries

100 g raspberries

honey to taste

Wash all the fruit and berries. Cut the melon in half, remove the seeds, peel and place the flesh in a blender with the rest of the ingredients. Blend until smooth.

Serve with whole blueberries.

TIP: Use cloudberries instead of blueberries and increase the amount of raspberries to 200 g.

Melon is related to cucumber and is suitable for making smoothies because of the high water content. Choose one that feels heavy and smells sweet around the base of the stalk.

STRAWBERRY & BASIL

2 glasses

350 g strawberries

6 basil leaves

200 ml water

syrup to taste

4 ice cubes

Wash the strawberries and basil leaves. Destalk the strawberries. Blend all the ingredients until smooth.

Serve with basil leaves.

TIP: Replace the basil with other fresh herbs, e.g. lemon balm, mint, lemongrass or a little rosemary. Only use the soft leaves.

Basil is not only used in food, but in liqueurs, cough mixtures and perfume. It was a symbol of hate to the ancient Romans, but the meaning has changed over the years, and in Italy today it symbolises love. Young Italian women put it in their hair as a sign that they are looking for love, and it is sure to attract men by the sweet smell.

RASPBERRY & PEARS

2 glasses

3 ripe Conference pears

250 g raspberries

200 ml ice water

honey to taste

Wash the pears and raspberries. Peel, quarter and core the pears. Place in a blender, add raspberries and water. Blend until smooth. Add honey to taste.

Serve with raspberries.

TIP: For a more liquid smoothie, juice the pears and only add 100 ml of water. Vary with a few pieces of mango.

Pears contain twice as much fibre as apples, but they keep less well. Buy unripe pears and keep them in the fridge. Store the pears together with apples, which emit a gas that cause the pears to ripen faster.

MANGO & CHILLI

2 glasses

2 large mangos

¼ red chilli

200 ml ice water

Peel the mango and dice, remember it has a large stone. Add the water and chopped chilli, membranes and seeds removed. Blend until smooth.

Serve with chillies.

TIP: Add less chilli if you do not like it strong, but do try a little. Even a small amount enhances the flavour. Just add more if you like it.

Chilli stimulates metabolism. The strength of different chillies varies, so be careful. Among the most common are jalapeño, habanero, tabasco and canario. You can buy dried chillies that work almost just as well as fresh, but be careful since the seeds are often included.

POMEGRANATE & GRAPEFRUIT

2 glasses

2 pomegranates

2 blood grapefruits

2 oranges

Wash all the fruit (including the citrus peel to get rid of pesticide residues). Cut the pomegranates in half and extract the juice. Peel the grapefruits and discard the membranes, pith and peel. Press the oranges. Blend until smooth.

Serve on the rocks and dilute it with a little water if it is too intense.

TIP: Just press the grapefruit if you do not want to remove the pith and membranes.

One grapefruit contains more than the daily recommended intake of vitamin C for adults. Pink or red grapefruits are sweeter than the standard yellow. Grapefruits do not grow in the wild, they were discovered in the 18th century in a West-Indian citrus plantation

BLUEBERRY & PEAR

2 glasses

2 pears

½ lemon

200 g blueberries

200 ml water

honey to taste

Peel, quarter and core the pears. Press the lemon and make sure no seeds end up in the smoothie. Blend all the ingredients until smooth.

Serve with fresh blueberries.

Blueberries are extremely nutritious. They contain antioxidants such as ascorbic acid and lutein.
Blueberry tea has been used as a natural remedy to relieve stomach pains and improve eyesight and memory.
Use frozen blueberries if you cannot find fresh ones.

REDCURRANT & MANGO

2 glasses

200 g redcurrants

100 g strawberries

1 mango

1 apple

Rinse the berries and fruit. Destalk the strawberries and the currants. Dice the apple and pass through a masticating or centrifugal juicer. Peel the mango and dice, remember there is large stone inside. Blend all the ingredients until smooth.

TIP: Use good-quality commercial apple juice with no additives if you do not have time to make your own.

Wild and cultivated currants can be used for making wine.

ORANGE & BANANA

2 glasses

2 bananas

4 oranges

½ lemon

Wash all the fruit. Peel the bananas and place in the blender. Press the oranges and lemon, making sure not to include any seeds, they will add a bitter taste. Blend until smooth.

Serve with lemon balm.

TIP: Add a few strawberries or raspberries for added colour and taste.

Oranges originally came from China. These days they are cultivated on all continents. Make a medicinal orange soup against the common cold by steeping one tablespoon chopped ginger, two tablespoons honey and a handful of raisins in half a litre of water. Refrigerate overnight and blend with the juice of one orange and two lemons.

RASPBERRY & BLUEBERRY

2 glasses

½ banana

250 g raspberries

200 g blueberries

200 ml ice water

honey or fructose to taste

Wash all the fruit and berries properly. Peel the banana. Blend until smooth.

Serve with fresh berries.

TIP: Use yoghurt instead of water for a classic blueberry and raspberry smoothie.

Raspberries are clusters of many small, individual berries that each contains a seed.

KIWI & BANANA

2 glasses

2 oranges

2 kiwis

1 banana

100 ml water

Wash all the fruit. Press the oranges. Peel and chop the kiwi, peel the bananas and blend all the ingredients until smooth.

TIP: Dilute with water if the smoothie becomes too thick.

The mini bananas sold in shops seem to have no other purpose than being attractive to young children. They look nice, but are no different from regular bananas.

MANGO & GINGER

2 glasses

2 mangos

3 cm (1 inch) fresh ginger

3 apples or 200 ml apple juice

Wash all the fruit. Dice the apples and juice. Peel the mango and dice, remember the large stone inside. Grate the ginger (including the peel) using a fine grater. Blend all the ingredients until smooth.

TIP: Add a little water if the smoothie is turning too thick. Add some chilli powder or fresh chilli for extra bite. If you are buying your apple juice ready-made, do not forget it should be of good quality, freshly made and additive-free.

Mango and ginger are popular ingredients in Indian food. Ginger originally came from China, but spread to Asia and Africa in ancient times. Ginger is both the name of the perennial plant and the root we use for seasoning.

STRAWBERRY & PINEAPPLE

2 glasses

200 g strawberries

½ pineapple

200 ml ice water

½ lime

Wash all the fruit carefully. Destalk the strawberries. Cut the pineapple in half, remove the leaves, peel and the hard core. Place the pineapple, strawberries and water in the blender. Cut the lime in half and squeeze out the juice, making sure to avoid the seeds, they add a bitter taste. Blend until thick and smooth.

TIP: Try another version by juicing pineapples and strawberries. Skip the water and pass the ingredients through a juicer instead.

Pineapples are sweet and excellent in desserts. If you are using pineapple in desserts that include cream and gelatine, it is best to add it as close to serving as possible since it contains a substance, bromeline, which prevents gelatine from setting.

KIWI & MANGO

2 glasses

2 oranges

3 kiwis

1 mango

100 ml ice water

Wash all the fruit. Press the oranges. Peel and chop the kiwi. Peel the mango and dice, remember there is a large stone inside. Blend until smooth.

TIP: When mangos are in season you can freeze them in batches in plastic bags. It is cheaper and better to use frozen fruit out of season than eating unripe fruit that has been stored for a long time and treated with preservatives. Fresh is always best, but fruit that is frozen directly after harvesting is fine too.

Until the 1960s, kiwis were called 'Chinese gooseberries'. Kiwis are usually imported from New Zealand, but are also in season in the Mediterranean between November and April. Ripe kiwis yield to light pressure. Watch out for very soft ones, they tend to taste bad..

MANGO & LEMON BALM

2 glasses

2 mangos

6 lemon balm leaves

200 ml water

Peel the mango and dice, remember there is a large stone inside. Chop the lemon balm and blend with the mango and water until smooth.

TIP: You can use lemon balm extract instead of the leaves.

Lemon balm is cultivated, but can be found in the wild too.

COCONUT & PINEAPPLE

2 glasses

½ pineapple

1 banana

100 ml coconut milk

½ lime

honey

4 ice cubes

Wash all the fruit carefully. Cut the pineapple in half, remove the leaves, peel and coarse centre. Cut the lime in half and squeeze out the juice. Avoid the seeds, they add a bitter taste. Peel the banana. Place the pineapple, banana, lime juice, coconut milk and ice cubes in the blender. Mix until thick and smooth. Add honey to taste.

Serve with coconut and pineapple on the side.

TIP: Always buy unsweetened coconut milk without additives and short best before date.

One of the great holiday classics is the Piña Colada. It is made with rum, pineapple and coconut. Make it by mixing 60 ml (2 oz) light rum, 30 ml (1 oz) coconut milk and 90 ml (3 oz) pineapple juice – but a smoothie is the healthier choice!

RASPBERRY & MANGO

2 glasses

1 mango

250 g raspberries

200 ml water

½ lime

honey to taste

Wash the mango and raspberries carefully. Peel the mango and dice, remember there is a large stone inside. Press the lime and make sure to avoid the seeds, they add a bitter taste. Blend all the ingredients until smooth.

TIP: Try to add a small pinch of chilli powder or a little chopped chilli.

Raspberries are full of an unusual form of antioxidant that cannot be found in any other food.
Buy raspberries that are evenly coloured and remember that they only keep for a couple of days.

BLACKCURRANT & GRAPEFRUIT

2 glasses

1 pear

1 grapefruit

200 g blackcurrants

100 g raspberries

100 ml ice water

Wash all the fruit. Rinse the berries. Peel the pears, quarter them and remove the cores. Peel the grapefruit and discard the pith, membranes and peel. Blend all the ingredients until smooth. Serve with blackcurrants on a cocktail stick

TIP: Add a few ice cubes instead of water for a more icy result.

Blackcurrants contain antioxidants that are said to be good for the eyesight, but they are rich in vitamin C too, as well as vitamins, fibres and folic acid.

MELON & RASPBERRY

2 glasses

1 honeydew melon

250 g raspberries

½ lime

4 ice cubes

Wash the fruit and berries and leave them to dry. Cut the melon in half, remove the seeds and peel and add to the blender. Cut the lime in half and press the juice straight into the blender making sure to avoid the seeds, they add a bitter taste. Add the raspberries and ice cubes and mix until thick and smooth.

Serve with raspberries or slices of melon on the side.

TIP: Add 1 banana for a thicker result.

Up to 200 bananas can grow on one plant.
Bananas are not only a fruit, they are a herb and a berry too!

POMEGRANATE & WATERMELON

2 glasses

½ lime

2 pomegranates

¼ watermelon

4 ice cubes

Wash the fruit, including the melon.
Press the lime. Cut the pomegranates
in half and extract the juice. Cut the
watermelon in half, remove seeds and
peel, chop the flesh and place in the
blender with the ice cubes. Blend until
smooth.

TIP: The watermelon can be replaced
with honeydew or Galia melon.

Watermelons are not related to other melons, and you cannot find a ripe one by using your sense of smell
as you do with other melons. There is a certain amount of risk-taking involved when you purchase one.
Choose one that does not make a hollow sound when you tap it.

CHERRY & BLUEBERRY

2 glasses

2 apples

200 g cherries

1 banana

200 g blueberries

Wash all the fruit and berries. Remove the stalks from the apples, then dice the apples and extract the juice. Remove the stones from the cherries and peel the banana. Blend all the ingredients until smooth.

TIP: If you are in a hurry or do not have access to a juicer, you can use a good quality, additive-free commercial brand of apple juice instead.

The best apples are the ones you pick yourself or the local varieties that are available in the shops for a short period in the autumn. Shops tend to prefer imported brands from New Zealand or Argentina, talk to your local shop and ask them to stock local varieties in season in order to create a demand.

MANDARIN & PAPAYA

2 glasses

6 mandarins, satsumas or clementines

1 small papaya (ca. 300 g)

½ lemon

Wash all the fruit. Press the mandarins and lemon, making sure that no seeds are included, they add a bitter taste. Cut the papaya in half, peel it, discard the seeds and dice. Blend all the ingredients until smooth.

TIP: Add a little water if you find the taste too intense.

Mandarin is the generic name for clementines, satsumas and tangerines. Mandarins contain a lot of seeds and are therefore often replaced by seedless clementines or satsumas. The clementine is a cross between a mandarin and a Seville orange. The smaller, more smooth-skinned Satsuma is a Japanese variety. Tangerines look somewhat like a reddish orange..

WATERMELON, STRAWBERRY & LIME

2 glasses

10 strawberries

¼ medium-sized watermelon

1 lime

crushed ice

Destalk the strawberries. Cut the watermelon in half, remove the seeds and place the flesh in a blender. Add the lime juice and strawberries, and blend until smooth. You can also juice the watermelon and strawberries if you do not like to taste the pulp.

Serve with watermelon slices on the side.

TIP: Blend with plenty of ice on a hot summer day to make it more like a sorbet and serve with strawberries. Do not forget to place a spoon or a thick straw in the glass.

Watermelons contain 90 % water and make a refreshing juice.

PRUNE & ALMOND

2 glasses

3 apples

12 prunes, stoned

12 almonds

200 ml water

Wash the apples and quarter, core, dice and juice them. Blend the prunes, almonds, apple juice and water until smooth.

Serve with prunes on the side.

TIP: If you are pressed for time, use a good commercial brand of apple juice, preferably organic and additive-free.

Prunes are excellent as a mid-afternoon snack, or use them in porridge.
There are many other great dishes made with prunes; they are even used for making wine.

MANGO & PINEAPPLE

2 glasses

1 mango

½ pineapple

½ lime

200 ml water

Peel the mango and dice, remember there is a large stone inside. Cut the pineapple in half, remove the leaves, peel and remove the tough centre. Press the lime, making sure you avoid the seeds, they add a bitter taste. Blend all the ingredients until smooth.

Serve with mango slices on a cocktail stick.

TIP: Put the fruit through a juicer if you do not like to taste the pulp. Dilute with a little water if the taste is too intense.

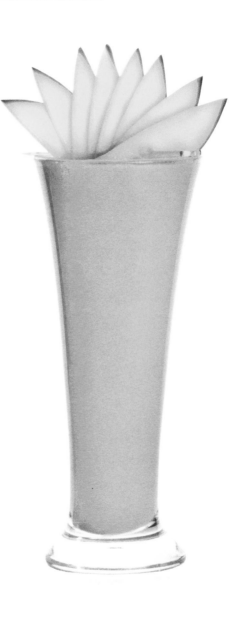

Limes are full of vitamin C. They are a popular cocktail ingredient and perfect for making smoothies. There are three types: the large, acidic, seedless one, a smaller, more aromatic one and then the 'real' lime, which is sweeter and resembles a clementine.

KIWI & ORANGE

2 glasses

½ banana

5 kiwis

2 oranges

1 grapefruit

100 ml water

Wash all the fruit. Peel the banana. Peel and chop the kiwi. Press the oranges and grapefruit and make sure not to include the seeds, they add a bitter taste. Blend all the ingredients until smooth.

TIP: Do not blend the kiwi for too long to avoid the seeds from breaking.

You can wash and eat the kiwi peel. It is soft and full of flavour, and you will not notice the hairs – it is good for you. Kiwis have a high vitamin C and E content. It does not blend well with dairy products, however. Mix it with other berries and tropical fruits.

STRAWBERRY & BANANA

2 glasses

2 oranges

2 bananas

250 g strawberries

100 ml water

Wash all the fruit. Press the oranges and peel the bananas. Blend all the ingredients until smooth.

TIP: Replace the strawberries with other tangy berries such as raspberries.

Most people know that oranges are full of vitamin C, but they contain many other nutrients that you will not get from an effervescent tablet. This orange berry contains plant substances and flavonoids. An orange a day gives a boost to your immune system and lowers blood pressure.

MELON & PASSION FRUIT

2 glasses

½ honeydew melon

¼ watermelon

6 passion fruits

½ lime

Wash all the fruit carefully. Remove the melon seeds, scoop out the flesh and place in a blender. Press the lime and add the juice to the blender. Pass the passion fruit through a sieve before adding it. Blend all the ingredients until smooth.

Serve with passion fruit or melon slices.

TIP: Use a juicer instead if you prefer.

Both the watermelon and the honeydew melon are members of the gourd, or cucurbitaceae family, but they are not related since they belong to different species.

NECTARINE & MANGO

2 glasses

2 nectarines

1 mango

2 oranges

½ lime

Wash the fruit. Press the oranges
and lime and make sure to avoid the
seeds, they add a bitter taste. Remove
the stones from the nectarines
and dice. Pell the mango and dice,
remember there is a large stone inside.
Blend all the ingredients until smooth.

TIP: Vary with 100 g of fresh or frozen
and thawed lingonberries (cowberries)
or cranberries.

Nectarines are peaches minus the downy peel. Nectarines and peaches may grow on the same tree,
and there is really no reason why they should be sold separately. Peaches have been cultivated in
China for over 4,000 years, but it was long believed they originated in Persia, thus the name.
The word nectarine comes from 'nectar' – the drink of the gods.

MELON & BANANA

2 glasses

1 honeydew melon

2 bananas

100 ml freshly pressed apple juice

1 lime

Peel the bananas and place in the blender. Cut the melon in half, remove the seeds and peel and place the flesh in the blender. Add lime juice making sure to avoid the pips, they add a bitter flavour. Add the freshly made apple juice. Blend all the ingredients until thick and smooth.

Serve with slices of melon.

TIP: Try other types of melon such as watermelon, Galia or cantaloupe.

Bananas are best kept in a separate bowl.
Many other fruits emit ethylene gas that causes them to ripen faster.

PAPAYA & MANDARIN

2 glasses

1 small papaya (ca. 300 g)

6 mandarins

½ lime

4 ice cubes

Wash all the fruit. Press the lime and mandarins, making sure you avoid the seeds, they add a bitter taste. Cut the papaya in half and remove the seeds. Scoop out the flesh, chop and place in a blender with fresh lime juice, mandarin juice and ice cubes. Blend all the ingredients until smooth.

Serve with papaya slices.

TIP: Papaya seeds are pretty, so sprinkle some on the smoothie to decorate. They are not bad for you but they do not taste that great either ...

Papaya is a tall plant that contains papain, a substance used to make drugs for digestive problems.
Some say it may help you to lose weight.

RHUBARB & STRAWBERRY

2 glasses

2 apples

2 rhubarb stalks

200 g strawberries

2–3 tsp honey or vanilla-flavoured icing sugar

Wash the fruit and berries. Dice the apples and pass through a centrifugal or masticating juicer. Peel and chop the rhubarb, discard the leaves and roots. Simmer the rhubarb and fresh apple juice on low heat for 5–6 minutes until the rhubarb has turned soft. Cool and blend with the strawberries and honey until smooth.

TIP: Add 150 g vanilla-flavoured quark cheese or vanilla yoghurt for a milder version.

Rhubarb leaves contain oxalic acid, which is toxic. There is little risk of consuming it by eating the stalk, but you should use the young plants in early summer to avoid it. The oxalic acid disappears with cooking, but do not use an aluminium cooking vessel since oxalic acid reacts with aluminium. Pick or buy rhubarb in the summer and freeze for a ready supply all year.

PEACH & RASPBERRY

2 glasses

2 oranges

4 ripe peaches

200 g raspberries

2 tbsp vanilla quark cheese

Wash the fruit and berries. Press the oranges. Halve and core the peaches and dice. Place all the ingredients in a blender and blend until smooth. Pass through a fine mesh for an even smoother texture.

Serve with peach slices on the side.

TIP: Use nectarines if peaches are not available.

The skin of peaches is furry and they can grow on the same tree as nectarines. Always buy ripe peaches, they do not ripen after harvesting, and they do not keep for more than a couple of days!gar!

MELON & GOJI BERRIES

2 glasses

1 honeydew melon
4 tsp dried goji berries
4 tsp dried cranberries
1 lime

Soak the goji berries and cranberries for an hour before use. Blend them with water until smooth. Wash the melon and cut it in half, remove the seeds and peel. Add the flesh to the blender. Cut the lime in half and add the juice to the other ingredients, but make sure to avoid the seeds, they add a bitter taste. Blend until smooth.

TIP: Vary with watermelon.

One single goji berry contains more vitamin C than two oranges. Just imagine what a couple of goji berries can do for your smoothie! They also contain vital amino acids, iron, calcium, selenium and zinc.

APPLE, PINEAPPLE & GINGER

2 glasses

½ pineapple

5 apples

2–3 cm (1 inch) ginger

Cut the pineapple in half, remove the leaves, peel and remove the tough centre. Dice. Halve the apples, remove the stalks and dice. Slice the ginger and put the slices and apples into a juicer. Transfer the juice to a blender, add pineapple chunks and blend until thick and smooth. Serve on ice with ginger and green herbs for garnish.

TIP: Pass all the ingredients through the juicer for a more liquid smoothie.

Most people know that cucumber is 99 % water, and that watermelons are 90 % water surprises no one, but did you know that apples are 85 % water? This does not mean they do not contain masses of nutrients and fibre, quite the reverse!

BLACKCURRANT & STRAWBERRY

2 glasses

250 g blackcurrants

200 g strawberries

200 ml fresh apple juice

1 tsp vanilla-flavoured icing sugar

ice cubes

Wash all the berries. Blend all the ingredients until thick and smooth.

Serve with a few blackcurrants.

TIP: Mix in 1 tbsp bran for some natural fibre. You cannot taste or feel the bran in a smoothie.

Vanilla tastes nice, but this spice arrived in Europe for a completely different reason. It was considered an aphrodisiac, which of course made it very popular in Europe in the 18th century. Men went so far as to flavour their pipe tobacco with vanilla seeds.

PLUM & ROSEHIP

2 glasses

6 yellow plums

2 tbsp rosehip powder

½ banana

2 apples

1 passion fruit

½ lemon

Wash all the fruit, including the banana. Cut the apples in half, remove the stalks, dice and pass through a juicer. Remove the stones from the plums and chop. Cut the passion fruit in half, scoop out the flesh and pass through a sieve to remove the seeds. Peel the bananas and slice. Press the lime. Blend everything until thick and smooth.

TIP: Try goji berries instead of rosehip powder. Any colour plum will do.

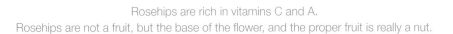

Rosehips are rich in vitamins C and A.
Rosehips are not a fruit, but the base of the flower, and the proper fruit is really a nut.

PEAR & PASSION FRUIT

2 glasses

4 pears

2 apples

½ banana

3 passion fruits

½ lime

Wash all the fruit. Cut the apples in half and quarter the pears, remove the stalks and dice. Peel the lime and dice. Cut the passion fruits in half and scoop out the flesh. Alternate apples, pears, lime and passion fruit in the juicer. Pour the juice into the blender, add banana and blend until smooth. Serve on ice with a passion fruit wedge and herb on the side.

TIP: Scoop out ½ passion fruit and sprinkle over the smoothie for an attractive effect.

Passion fruit is in fact a berry. You can grow them yourself. Buy a passion fruit, separate the seeds from the flesh and plant them in a pot. After a few months you will have a green seedling, which will in time grow to a 15-metre-high climbing plant. It needs to be kept warm in the winter, but you can put it outdoors in the summer to allow it to be pollinated and grow berries.

REDCURRANT & MANGO

2 glasses

200 g redcurrants

100 g strawberries

1 mango

1 apple

Rinse the berries and fruit, destalk the strawberries, remove the stalks from the currants. Dice the apple and pass it through a masticating or centrifugal juicer. Peel the mango and dice, remember there is a stone inside. Blend all the ingredients until smooth.

TIP: Use a good-quality, preservative-free commercial brand of apple juice if you are in a rush.

You can make rather good wine from redcurrants.

2 glasses

2 apples
100 g strawberries
1 banana
100 g raspberries
100 g blueberries

Wash all the fruit. Rinse the berries. Dice the apples and pass through a masticating or centrifugal juicer. Destalk the strawberries, peel the banana and blend all the ingredients together with the apple juice until smooth.

Serve with raspberries and blueberries on a cocktail stick.

TIP: Replace the apple juice with 300 ml plain yoghurt for a more substantial smoothie. Add honey or vanilla honey to taste.

Raspberries grow wild on lime-free soils in northern Europe.

PEAR & GINGER

2 glasses

2 soft pears

3 cm (1 inch) ginger

1 orange

½ lime

100 ml water

Peel, quarter and core the pears. Peel and grate the fresh ginger. Press the orange and lime, and make sure to avoid the seeds, they add a bitter taste. Blend until thick and smooth.

TIP: Make a delicious juice by passing everything through a juicer instead. Remember to peel the lime and the orange, but not the pears, before processing them. Alternate soft and hard fruit in the machine.

In the 13th century, the medical faculty at the University of Salerno said the following about the almost magic properties of ginger: 'Eat ginger and you will love and be loved like a youngster.' The Portuguese took this to heart when they started to cultivate ginger in West Africa. They hoped it would do a lot of good to the 'slave stock', but the effect has not been proven.

BLACK & RED CURRANTS

2 glasses

Blackcurrants:	Redcurrants:
200 g blackcurrants	200 g redcurrants
2 apples	2 pears
4 strawberries	½ banana
1 tsp honey	1 tsp honey

This is in fact two smoothies in one. It is as easy to serve it in layers as it is to mix the two.

Wash all the fruit and berries. Cut the apples in half and quarter the pears, remove the stalks and dice. Juice the pears first and then the apples, but keep the two separated if you are going to make a layered smoothie. Peel and cut the banana. Destalk the strawberries.

Pour apple juice, blackcurrants and strawberries into a beaker and blend until smooth. Add honey to taste (optional).

Pour pear juice, redcurrants and banana in another beaker and blend until smooth.

Pour the blackcurrant smoothie in the glass first, then slowly spoon a redcurrant layer on top. Sprinkle with black and redcurrants.

TIP: ... or just blend all the ingredients.

Have you ever smelled a blackcurrant bush? It smells just as good as the berries.
You can make delicious tea or cordial from the leaves.

PAPAYA & PASSION FRUIT

2 glasses

2 apples

1 small papaya (ca. 300 g)

1 banana

2 passion fruits

Wash the fruit. Dice the apples. Cut the papaya in half, remove the seeds and dice the flesh. Pass the papaya and apples through a juicer alternating papaya and apples. Transfer the juice to the blender, add passion fruit and banana, and blend quickly.

TIP: For a smoother result, remove the passion fruit seeds by pouring a little water inside the fruit and mix it with the pulp until it the seeds separate from the pulp. Pass through a sieve and use only the liquid for the smoothie.

Nutritious papain, which relieves digestive problems, is extracted from papayas.
The unripe fruit is slashed with a knife and the liquid is collected.

CRANBERRY & PEAR

2 glasses

200 g cranberries

3 soft, sweet pears

1 orange

Wash all the fruit and berries. Press the orange. Cut the pears in half, remove cores and stalks and dice. Mix all the ingredients until thick and smooth.

TIP: Pass all the ingredients through a juicer for a less pulpy smoothie and add a little water if it is too strong.

Just like lingonberries (cowberries) and cloudberries, cranberries contain benzoic acid, a natural preservative.

YOGHURT & BREAKFAST SMOOTHIES

BLACKBERRY & VANILLA

2 glasses

½ vanilla pod

4 tsp honey

200 g blackberries

100 g blueberries

300 ml plain yoghurt

50 ml water

Split the vanilla pod and scrape the seeds into a small saucepan with 50 ml water. Add the pod and boil for 2–3 minutes. Add the honey just before removing from the heat, cool and remove the vanilla pod. Blend all the ingredients until smooth.

TIP: Make a large quantity of vanilla honey, it keeps for about 2 weeks in the fridge and can be used to flavour any type of smoothie.

According to one theory, the darker the berries, the more nutritious they are. Blackberries are the darkest of them all. They contain large amounts of potassium, which is said to protect against cancer and cardiovascular disease. Only pick very ripe blackberries – they taste bad if they are picked too early. Most blackberries do not ripen until September/October.

BLACKCURRANT & QUARK CHEESE

2 glasses

200 g blackcurrants

100 g raspberries

200 g vanilla quark cheese

Rinse the berries. Set aside
100 g currants for garnish.
Mix all the ingredients until
smooth.

TIP: Use vanilla yoghurt instead
of quark cheese for variation.

Quark cheese is made by warming soured milk and then straining it.
Quark usually has about the same fat content as yoghurt and has no added salt.

VANILLA & APPLE

2 glasses

2 apples

200 g vanilla quark cheese

½ vanilla pod

2 tsp honey

Wash and dice the apples and pass through a juicer. Split the vanilla pod and scrape out the seeds from one half. Pour apple juice, quark cheese and vanilla seeds into the blender and blend briefly. This type of smoothie should not be processed too long, or it will become too thin.

TIP: Use manuka honey if you can get hold of it, it is delicious. Store the leftover vanilla pod in a sugar-filled jar with a tight-fitting lid.

Nothing may have been added or removed for honey to be sold as honey; it must be completely 'clean'. Honey can be made from virtually any nectar-producing plant. Manuka honey comes from the manuka bush, which grows in New Zealand. It is considered to be especially nutritious since it contains many antioxidants that can help relieve the effects of the common cold or food poisoning and it is said that it can be used to heal wounds.

LINGONBERRY & CARDAMOM

2 glasses

200 g lingonberries (cowberries)

1 banana

150 g vanilla quark cheese

1 pinch cardamom

Wash all the fruits and berries. Blend all the ingredients until smooth.

Serve with lingonberries.

TIP: If you cannot find fresh lingonberries, replace them with frozen cranberries, or try cinnamon instead of cardamom.

Lingonberries are rich in vitamin C and have been used as a source, sometimes the only source, of vitamin C in Scandinavia where it frequently accompanies meatballs, black pudding, herring and many other dishes.

LINGONBERRY & CARDAMOM

2 glasses

200 g lingonberries (cowberries)
1 banana
150 g vanilla quark cheese
1 pinch cardamom

Wash all the fruits and berries. Blend all the ingredients until smooth.

Serve with lingonberries.

TIP: If you cannot find fresh lingonberries, replace them with frozen cranberries, or try cinnamon instead of cardamom.

Lingonberries are rich in vitamin C and have been used as a source, sometimes the only source, of vitamin C in Scandinavia where it frequently accompanies meatballs, black pudding, herring and many other dishes.

OAT MILK & RASPBERRY

2 glasses

250 g raspberries

200 ml oat milk

1 banana

Blend all the ingredients until smooth. Pass through a sieve for an ever smoother drink.

Serve with a few raspberries.

Even the ancient Greeks recommended oatmeal porridge as an easily digested remedy against stomach problems. The fibres are removed from oat milk for a smoother consistency.

BLUEBERRY & VANILLA

2 glasses

200 g blueberries

100 g raspberries

300 ml plain yoghurt

vanilla-flavoured icing sugar

Rinse the berries and leave them to dry. Blend all the ingredients until smooth and add vanilla-flavoured sugar to taste. It is delicious.

Serve with a few lemon balm leaves and sprinkle a few blueberries over the smoothie.

Vanilla was first introduced in Spain via Aztec drinking chocolate before it was spread to the rest of Europe. In 1602, Queen Elizabeth I's apothecary discovered it was perfect for flavouring sweets, but it would take another 100 years before vanilla became famous throughout Europe for a completely different reason. It was marketed as an aphrodisiac.

STRAWBERRY & LINSEED

2 glasses

3 tbsp linseeds

200 g strawberries

1 banana

200 ml plain yoghurt

Wash all the fruit. Soak the linseeds or use crushed linseeds. Destalk the strawberries, peel the banana and blend until smooth and creamy.

Sprinkle with linseeds.

TIP: Add some cold-pressed linseed oil for an additional energy-boost.

The laxative and beneficial properties of linseeds have been known since the 16th century or longer. But it is important not to overdose.

ALMOND & BANANA

2 glasses

2 bananas

200 ml plain yoghurt

2 tbsp almond butter

1 tsp vanilla-flavoured icing sugar

Peel the bananas and add yoghurt, almond butter and vanilla-flavoured icing sugar. Blend until smooth.

TIP: If you cannot find almond butter in your local health food shop, process some peeled almonds and a little water until smooth before adding the other ingredients, or use a commercial brand of almond milk.

Almond butter should not be confused with peanut butter, but it is just as tasty and a lot healthier. You can make butter from other nuts too, hazelnuts for example.

STRAWBERRY & VANILLA

2 glasses

200 g strawberries

150 g vanilla quark cheese

50 ml milk

Destalk the strawberries. Blend
with the quark cheese and milk until
smooth and fluffy. Garnish with fresh
strawberries and fresh mint.

TIP: Replace the quark cheese
with yoghurt and a little extra vanilla
flavouring. I usually add 2 tbsp of
wheat bran to keep my stomach
in trim.

Fibre-rich wheat bran is an excellent breakfast cereal. It is made from the outer husk of the wheat berry,
which means that it contains no gluten. However, it cannot always be absolutely guaranteed gluten-free
since it may be contaminated by other parts of the wheat berry.

SUMMER BERRY & YOGHURT

2 glasses

100 g strawberries

100 g raspberries

100 g blueberries

300 ml vanilla yoghurt

honey to taste

Rinse the berries and leave to dry. Blend the berries and 150 ml yoghurt until smooth. Pour the remaining yoghurt into the glasses so that the white yoghurt is unevenly distributed along the inside of the glass, then add the berry-yoghurt mixture. You should please the eye as well as the palate. Alternatively, pour in the yoghurt and berry mixture in layers.

TIP: Make your own vanilla yoghurt by adding vanilla seeds, vanilla honey, vanilla syrup or home-made vanilla-flavoured icing sugar to plain yoghurt and chill. Use vanilla-flavoured quark cheese to make a dessert smoothie.

Lingonberries, blueberries, raspberries, cloudberries and brambles are only some of several hundred wild species.

PRUNE & CINNAMON

2 glasses

12 prunes, without stones

300 ml plain yoghurt

1 pinch cinnamon

honey

Wash the prunes and soak for half an hour. Blend all the ingredients until smooth. Add a little honey to taste.

Serve with chopped prunes.

TIP: Vary with a few spoonfuls of goji berries for an extra vitamin boost.

Prunes are in fact dried plums. They were originally cultivated in the Syrian capital, Damascus.

VANILLA & RASPBERRY

2 glasses

½ vanilla pod
200 g raspberries
200 ml plain yoghurt
100 ml full fat milk
3 tbsp liquid honey
(preferably organic macadamia honey)

Split the vanilla pod down the middle and scrape the seeds into a small saucepan along with 50 ml water. Add the pod and boil for 2–3 minutes. Mix in the honey just before removing the saucepan from the heat, cool the vanilla honey and remove the vanilla pod. Blend all the ingredients until smooth. Dip the glasses in melted chocolate and leave to set. Pour in the smoothie.

TIP: Make a large batch of vanilla-flavoured honey if you like the taste, it keeps for about two weeks in the fridge. Use it to flavour smoothies and yoghurt.

Yoghurt was used as far back as 2000 B.C. by the Indo-Iranian culture.
Yoghurt and honey is mentioned as food for the gods.

BLACKCURRANT & OATMEAL

2 glasses

250 g blackcurrants

2 tbsp oatmeal

1 tbsp wheat bran

1 tbsp crushed linseeds

200 ml plain yoghurt

3 tbsp maple syrup

Rinse the berries. Blend all the ingredients until smooth.

TIP: If blackcurrants are not in season, use frozen berries, or replace them with any other berry or the yoghurt with apple juice.

White currants are exactly the same berries as redcurrants, but without the red pigment. There are yellow ones too. White and yellow currants are suitable for making currant wine.

VANILLA, APPLE & HONEY

2 glasses

200 ml plain yoghurt

200 ml Greek yoghurt

1 apple

½ vanilla pod

3 tbsp liquid honey
(preferably acacia honey)

50 ml water

Wash and cut the apple in half, peel, remove the core and dice. Split the vanilla pod down the middle and scrape the seeds into a small saucepan with 50 ml water and the apple chunks. Add the vanilla pod and boil for 2–3 minutes. Mix in the honey just before removing the saucepan from the heat, cool the vanilla honey and remove the vanilla pod. Blend all the ingredients until smooth. Refrigerate quickly before serving to bring out the vanilla and honey flavours.

TIP: Omit the Greek yoghurt for a more liquid smoothie.

The Mexican Totona tribe have a story about the fertility goddess Xanath who fell in love with a mortal man. Since she could not love him, she turned herself into a vanilla orchid in order to be close to him. This was how vanilla came to be. The Totona first learned how to use vanilla, and later the Spaniards picked it up from the Aztecs.

VEGETABLE
SMOOTHIES

CARROT & PINEAPPLE

2 glasses

6 carrots (300 ml fresh carrot juice)

½ pineapple

½ lime

4 ice cubes

Wash and brush the carrots and pass through a juicer. Refrigerate the carrot juice, which tastes best cold. Wash and cut the pineapple in half, remove the leaves, peel and remove the tough centre. Place the pineapple flesh, carrot juice and ice in a blender. Cut the lime in half and squeeze out the juice. Make sure to avoid the seeds, they add a bitter taste. Blend until smooth.

Serve with a slice of pineapple or carrots.

TIP: Pass all the ingredients through a juicer if you prefer a more liquid mixture. Leftover pineapple can be kept in an airtight plastic bag in the freezer.

Carrots are the most vitamin-rich of all vegetables. They are beset kept without the tops in a plastic bag in the fridge or in a cool larder. The carrot tops leach nutrients from the carrots.

CUCUMBER, APPLE & LIME

2 glasses

1 cucumber

3 apples

½ lime

Wash all the fruit and greens. Peel and slice the cucumber. Cut the apples in half, remove the stalks and seeds, they add a bitter taste to the smoothie. Dice the apples. Alternate cucumber and apples in the juicer. Squeeze the juice from the lime straight into the glass.

Serve with apple and cucumber slices.

TIP: Vary by adding celery or wheatgrass.

The cucumber originated in India. It is in fact a fruit. It contains as much as 96 % water. Because of its mild taste, many think it lacks nutrients, but it does contain vitamin C.

BEETROOT & CHILLI

2 glasses

2 raw mini beetroots

2 apples

½ red chilli

Wash and brush the beetroots, apples and chilli carefully. Dice the beetroots and apples. Remove the seeds and membranes from the chilli unless you want it really spicy. Run all the ingredients through a juicer. Cool with plenty of ice in a large shaker or stir it with ice in the glass. Serve immediately.

TIP: Clean the juicer from chilli or other strong tasting ingredients by immediately afterwards juicing a lemon (without the pith). It removes the strong flavours naturally. But you still need to wash the juicer in order to save a great deal of trouble later.

Small beetroots are easier to handle since you do not need to cut them and thereby stain your cutting board. Remember that beetroot greens are very nutritious. Save and make a beetroot soup with the greens.

AVOCADO & MANGO

2 glasses

2 avocados

1 mango

½ lemon

200 ml water

Cut the avocado in half, remove the stone and scoop out the flesh with a spoon. Peel the mango and dice, remember there is a large stone inside. Cut the lemon in half and squeeze out the juice into the mixer. Make sure not to include the seeds, they add a bitter taste to the smoothie. Blend until smooth and creamy.

TIP: If you have to keep half an avocado, leave the stone inside, squeeze a little lemon over the surface and cover in cling film. Refrigerate and eat within 24 hours.

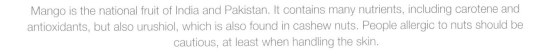

Mango is the national fruit of India and Pakistan. It contains many nutrients, including carotene and antioxidants, but also urushiol, which is also found in cashew nuts. People allergic to nuts should be cautious, at least when handling the skin.

PEAR, KIWI & BROCCOLI

2 glasses

2 pears

1 apple

2 kiwis

½ banana

5 broccoli florets

Wash all the fruit and greens. Cut the apple and pears in half, remove the stalks and dice. Break off a few broccoli florets. Put the apples, pears and broccoli alternately in a juicer. Peel the banana and kiwi. Pour the juice into the blender and blend with the kiwi and banana, but not too long since the kiwi seeds may break and add a bitter taste to the smoothie.

TIP: Start with a small amount of broccoli if you are unsure whether you like it or not. I was surprised to find how well it went with the rest of the ingredients, but you should go easy on it.

Broccoli comes from Italy. The name derives from 'brocco', an Italian word meaning 'fragile branch'.

BEETROOT & CARROT

2 glasses

3 raw mini beetroots
5 carrots
3 tart, green apples
(e.g. Granny Smith)

Brush and wash the beetroots, carrots and apples carefully. Dice everything and put through a juicer. Serve immediately on ice in a large glass.

TIP: Add 1 celery stalk for an extra vitamin boost.

Carrots contain plenty of beta-carotene, which forms vitamin A in the body. The so-called mini or baby carrot is a peeled carrot that has been cut into bite-size pieces. It was produced as a healthy alternative to fries in fast food restaurants. Carrots are healthy food, but not, which you often hear, a cure for bad eyesight. This myth derives from the fact that the lack of vitamin A can affect your eye-sight.

STRAWBERRY & BEETROOT

2 glasses

¼ raw mini beetroot

½ lime

200 g strawberries

200 ml vanilla yoghurt

Brush and wash the beetroots, rinse the berries and lime. Peel and grate the beetroot finely or pass it through a juicer. Press the lime with a citrus press and pour the fresh juice into the blender. Destalk the strawberries and blend everything until smooth.

TIP: The beetroot adds a very interesting flavour. It is full of antioxidants and adds a lovely colour to this otherwise drab-looking smoothie.

Beetroots contain calcium, vitamin C, iron, magnesium, phosphor and manganese.
They are also said to cleanse the liver, gut and aid kidney function.

CARROT, ORANGE & CHILLI

2 glasses

6 carrots

2 oranges

½ red chilli

Scrub and wash all the fruit and greens in lukewarm water. It is important to wash the citrus fruits too in order to prevent any pesticide residues entering the smoothie. Peel the carrots if necessary and slice. Peel and cut the oranges. Cut the chilli in half lengthwise and remove the seeds. Alternate chilli, carrots and orange in the juicer.

Serve immediately with slices of carrot on the side, or strips of chilli for the more adventurous.

TIP: When you need to clean the juicer from chilli or other strong tastes, juice a lemon (without the pith) straight after you have used it. It removes the strong flavours naturally.

You can become addicted to chilli because of the capsaicin that stimulates endorphin production in the body. Endorphins make you relaxed and relieve pain, so it is not strange you long for a bit of chilli every now and then.

BEETROOT & GARLIC

2 glasses

2 raw mini beetroots

2 apples

2 garlic cloves

½ lime

2 tsp honey

Rinse the fruit and greens. Peel the garlic cloves. Peel and cut up the lime. Dice the apples and beetroots, discarding the peel and core. Juice the beetroots, lime, garlic and apples. Pour 1 tsp honey at the bottom of the glass, pour on the juice and sweep it in one go.

TIP: Just add more garlic if you have got a cold, it may not taste very nice, but honey and garlic are supposed to work, at least it can't hurt …

Fresh garlic is a little milder and has not yet formed cloves.
Fresh garlic may increase fat metabolism and reduce sugar craving.

AVOCADO & PINEAPPLE

2 glasses

½ pineapple

1 avocado

½ lime

100 ml water

Cut the pineapple in half, remove the leaves and peel. Dice and pass through a juicer (or use ready-made juice). Cut the avocado in half, remove the stone and scoop out the flesh with a spoon. Add lime juice. Blend until thick and smooth.

TIP: Juice the pineapple before you mix in the avocado for a more liquid smoothie.

Find a ripe pineapple by trying to pull out one of the leaves at the bottom. It will come out easily if the pineapple is ripe, but it may also be overripe, so choose one that is not quite ripe yet and leave it for a few days at home.

AVOCADO & SPINACH

2 glasses

3 green apples

2 avocados

1 lime

50 g baby spinach

Wash all the fruit well. Peel, quarter and core the apples. Pass the apple chunks through a juicer. Cut the avocados in half, remove the stones and use a spoon to scoop out the flesh. Cut the lime in half and squeeze the juice straight into the blender, but make sure that no seeds are included, they add a bitter taste. Blend until smooth.

Garnish with baby spinach.

TIP: Use good-quality, freshly-made apple juice if you do not have time to make your own.

Avocado is a berry named for the Spanish *aguacate*, which in turn comes from the Aztec word *ahuacatl*, which means 'testicle' (referring to the shape). Throughout the ages, avocado has been considered an aphrodisiac. Apart from the alleged potency-enhancing properties and the good fatty acids, avocados have many other good properties. It is an old herbal remedy used externally to improve skin and hair.

BEETROOT & CELERY

2 glasses

2 raw mini beetroots

2 carrots

1 apple

1 stalk of celery

½ lime

Wash and scrub the greens and fruit well. Peel the lime, carrots, apple and celery. Pass everything through a juicer. Cool in a large shaker filled with ice or stir until chilled in a glass. Serve immediately.

The myth that carrots are good for the eyesight may derive from the claim that British Air Force pilots during WWII got better night vision from eating carrots since they suddenly seemed to hit more targets than they did before they started eating carrots. But the truth is probably that the cause was the advent of radar.

DESSERT SMOOTHIES

CHOCOLATE & MINT

2 glasses

4 scoops of good quality ice cream

200 ml milk

50 g dark chocolate, min. 50 %

a few drops of mint extract

Melt the chocolate in warm milk and leave to cool. Blend all the ingredients until smooth.

Serve with chocolate and mint.

TIP: If you happen to have a box of After Eights at home, you can use that, or replace the ice cream with mint chocolate ice cream.

The cocoa fruit resembles a 20-centimetre-long cucumber and contains almond-size seeds. The seeds are fermented and toasted and then crushed and ground to a paste from which 'cocoa butter' is made. When the fat has been pressed out of the beans, the residue is pulverized to make cocoa powder.

CHERRY & COCONUT

2 glasses

200 g cherries

150 g vanilla quark cheese

3 tbsp coconut milk

Wash the cherries and remove the stones. Blend the cherries, quark cheese and coconut milk until smooth. Add honey to taste.

TIP: Since cherries can be hard to find, you can use sweet cherries instead, or frozen cherries. Decorate the glass by dipping it in chocolate for an attractive visual effect. Or garnish with home-made chocolate figures.

The sweet cherry is a firmer, less juicy sub-species of the cherry.

CHOCOLATE & BANANA

2 glasses

2 bananas

3 scoops vanilla ice cream

100 ml milk

2 tsp cocoa powder

vanilla-flavoured icing sugar to taste

Wash and peel the bananas. Blend until smooth.

TIP: Bananas freeze well in resealable plastic bags. Use them when you are out of fresh ones.

Chocolate with high cocoa content has become fashionable, and the percentage is usually printed on the packaging. Cocoa contains antioxidants, vitamins and minerals and is supposed to be good for the heart. Apart from the cocoa, white chocolate contains exactly the same ingredients as brown chocolate.

WHITE CHOCOLATE & RASPBERRIES

2 glasses

50 g white chocolate

4 scoops of vanilla ice cream

200 g raspberries

3 tbsp milk

Powder the chocolate in the blender. Add milk, raspberries and vanilla ice cream and blend until smooth.

TIP: The best ice cream is home-made. If you do use a commercial brand, use a good quality one made from real vanilla and cream. Read the table of contents to make sure there are no unnecessary additives.

White 'chocolate' contains no cocoa powder.
The rest of the ingredients are identical to brown chocolate.

COFFEE & VANILLA

2 glasses

5 scoops of vanilla ice cream

200 ml milk

100 ml cold espresso or strong coffee

grated chocolate for garnish

Make a nice milkshake-smoothie by blending all the ingredients. Sprinkle with grated chocolate.

TIP: Add more coffee if you like the taste. Serve with a few coffee beans.

The word coffee comes from Arabic and means wine. When wine was banned in Muslim countries, coffee took its place as a social beverage.

CHOCOLATE & CHILLI

2 glasses

300 ml milk

3 scoops of ice cream

50 g dark chocolate

¼ red chilli

Heat the milk and add the chocolate. Stir until it has melted. Add 2–4 slices of chilli without the seeds and refrigerate. Remove the chilli slices before adding the ice cream. Blend until smooth. Garnish with chocolate twists. You make them by gently 'peeling' the edge of the chocolate with a potato peeler.

TIP: Chocolate and chilli is a great combo, but if you are not used to strong flavours, start with one or two slices of chilli.

If you are suffering from a sore throat, make a soothing hot infusion by mixing ½ tsp cinnamon with 1 tsp chopped, fresh ginger and ¼ tsp chopped red chilli. Sweeten with a little honey and add lemon or lime juice. It has been suggested that chilli aids weight reduction since it increases body temperature and thus the metabolic rate.

CHOCOLATE & VANILLA

2 glasses

200 g vanilla quark cheese

100 ml plain yoghurt

50 g dark chocolate

2 tbsp water

Melt the chocolate in a bain-marie and mix in 2 tbsp hot water. Add 3 tbsp quark cheese to prevent it from setting. Blend the chocolate cream with the other ingredients. For a pretty smoothie trickle chocolate cream on the inside of the glass, pour in the white mixture and drizzle chocolate cream on top.

TIP: If you like mint chocolate, add a couple of drops of mint extract to the cream or melt two After Eight wafers with the rest of the chocolate.

Vanilla derives from the Latin word for 'vagina' (because of the sheath-like vanilla pod). Perhaps this was enough to inspire the German doctor Bezaar Zimmeran in the 18th century to claim that vanilla unequalled as an aphrodisiac and a cure for impotence.

HAZELNUT & CHOCOLATE

2 glasses

100 g hazelnuts

50 g dark chocolate

1 banana

150 g vanilla ice cream

200 ml milk

Powder hazelnuts and dark chocolate. Peel the banana. Add cold milk and banana, and blend until smooth. Blend in the ice cream.

Pour into glasses and drizzle a little melted chocolate or chocolate sauce on top.

TIP: Health food shops sell 100 % pure hazelnut paste that can be used instead of ground hazelnuts.

The nutritious hazelnut has been appreciated and cultivated ever since the Middle Ages. These days they are often added to cakes and pastries.

COCONUT & CHOCOLATE

2 glasses

50 g dark chocolate

100 ml milk

1 banana

2 tbsp coconut milk

150 g vanilla ice cream

fresh or shredded coconut

Melt the chocolate in warm milk and leave to cool. Peel the banana. Add coconut milk and ice cream and blend until smooth. Grate a little fresh coconut on top, or use desiccated, shredded coconut.

Serve with fresh coconut on the side.

TIP: Always buy good quality chocolate with a minimum cocoa content of 50 % and make sure there are no unnecessary additives in the coconut milk and ice cream.

How do you break open a coconut? Prick a hole in each of the three 'eyes' at one end and pour out the liquid. Place the nut in a 200 °C oven for 20 minutes. Use the back of a large knife to tap around the middle of the nut. The shell will crack and break easily. Peel off the thin, brown layer with a potato peeler. Good luck!

POMEGRANATE & COCONUT

2 glasses

½ pomegranate

200 g strawberries

150 g vanilla quark cheese

100 ml coconut milk or cream

2 tsp coconut flakes

Wash the pomegranate and strawberries. Destalk the strawberries. Cut the pomegranate in half and extract the juice using a citrus press. Pour all the ingredients into a blender and blend until smooth.

Serve with a few pomegranate seeds.

TIP: Mix the smoothie with 100–200 g crushed ice to make a frozen smoothie.

The pomegranate has biblical roots. The First Book of Genesis describes how King Solomon's crown was inspired by a pomegranate. The top end really does look a little like a crown. Pomegranates are also mentioned in the Song of Songs where it is compared to the beauty of a woman, and the seeds are fertility symbols.

FRUITY COCKTAILS

STRAWBERRY MARGARITA

2 oz (60 ml) tequila

1 ½ oz (45 ml) lemon juice

½ oz (15 ml) simple syrup

6 fresh strawberries

1 lemon wedge

Frosted rim for garnish

Pour all the ingredients into a blender with crushed ice and mix them until 'half frozen' – stop before they turn into sorbet. Pour into a cocktail glass with a frosted rim.

Frosted Rim: Pour salt or sugar onto a saucer. Moisten the rim of the glass with the lime wedge and dip the upturned glass into the contents of the saucer.

Tequila must contain at least 51 % agave to be allowed the name tequila. The most exclusive tequila is made with 100 % agave and aged in oak barrels. However, don't use this sort of tequila for cocktails, it's better to drink it like a fine Scotch.

FROZEN MOJITO

2 oz (60 ml) light rum

1 oz (30 ml) lime juice

½ oz (15 ml) simple syrup

6–10 mint leaves

Pour all the ingredients into a blender. Blend briefly at high speed until smooth. Start with a small amount of crushed ice and add more until you get the desired thickness. Serve in a cocktail glass.

Mojito was one of Ernest Hemingway's favourite drinks during his time in Cuba. He used to enjoy them at La Bodeguita del Medio in Havana. The author is part of the reason why this Cuban drink has become so successful worldwide. This is the frozen form, which is almost as famous as the original. (The more mint leaves, the greener the Mojito.)

FROZEN BLACKBERRY DAIQUIRI

1 ½ oz (45 ml) golden rum

½ oz (15 ml) Crème de Mûre

5 blackberries

1 oz (30 ml) lemon juice

½ oz (15 ml) honey

Crushed ice

Pour all the ingredients into a blender. Blend briefly at high speed until smooth. Start with a small amount of crushed ice and add more until you achieve the desired thickness. Serve in a margarita glass and garnish with lemon balm.

Frozen Daiquiri is a common Daiquiri variation . Besides rum, lime juice and simple syrup, it contains crushed ice and fruit or berries. For a more intense flavour, add a matching liqueur, as we have done here.

FROZEN BLUEBERRY DAIQUIRI

1 oz (30 ml) light rum

1 oz (30 ml) blueberry liqueur

2 oz (60 ml) blueberries

1 oz (30 ml) lime juice

½ oz (15 ml) simple syrup

Crushed ice

Pour all the ingredients into a blender. Blend briefly at high speed until smooth. Start with a small amount of crushed ice and add more until you achieve the desired thickness. Serve in a margarita glass and garnish with lemon balm.

TIP! You can also try using home-made or a commercial brand of blueberry puree.

Nordic forest fruits meet the national spirit of Cuba and the summer is saved.

FROZEN BANANA DAIQUIRI

2 oz (60 ml) light rum

½ banana

1 oz (30 ml) lime or lemon juice

½ oz (15 ml) simple syrup

Crushed ice

Pour all the ingredients into a blender. Blend briefly at high speed until smooth. Start with a small amount of crushed ice and add more until you achieve the desired thickness. Serve in a margarita glass.

Daiquiri comes in a million versionsover and above the original cocktail of rum, citrus and sugar. Legendary bartender Constante made the Floridita restaurant famous with his own original version made with maraschino liqueur and crushed ice. For Mr. Hemingway he added grapefruit juice instead of sugar. Until this day, tourists and Cubans go on pilgrimages to the Floridita bar, where Daiquiris are said to taste better than anywhere else in the world.

FROZEN RASPBERRY DAIQUIRI

2 oz (60 ml) Bacardi Razz

8–10 raspberries

1 oz (30 ml) lime juice

½ oz (15 ml) simple syrup

Crushed ice

Pour all the ingredients into a blender. Blend briefly at high speed until smooth. Start with a small amount of crushed ice and add more until you achieve the desired thickness. Serve in a margarita glass and garnish with fresh raspberries.

The trick of mixing a perfect original Daiquiri is to squeeze the lime gently to avoid the bitter juice from the peel. Blend the drink for a few seconds only, no longer. If you're not very experienced, you can always mix a flavoured Daiquiri instead, like the next one, which is made with raspberries. You can't go wrong, and it's incredibly tasty!

FROZEN CHI CHI

2 oz (60 ml) vodka

1 oz (30 ml) thick coconut cream

1 ½ oz (45 ml) pineapple juice

Crushed ice

Pour all the ingredients into a blender. Blend briefly at high speed until smooth. Start with a small amount of crushed ice and add more until you achieve the desired thickness. Pour into a glass of your choice and garnish with a tropical touch.

TIP! If you are not a fan of coconut cream, try coconut liqueur or coconut syrup instead. Add half a banana for the right thickness.

Blue Hawaii made with curaçao and Chi Chi made with vodka are both Piña Colada variations.

RASPBERRY KISS

1 oz (30 ml) white crème de cacao

1 oz (30 ml) raspberry liqueur

1 oz (30 ml) double cream

Crushed ice

Pour all the ingredients into a blender. Blend briefly at high speed until smooth. Start with a small amount of crushed ice and add more until you achieve the desired thickness. Pour into a glass of your choice and garnish with fresh raspberries.

Raspberries grow wild all over Northern Europe, but they are also cultivated commercially all year round. If you're looking for wild raspberries, try to find them where the landscape is a bit rocky and around forest clearings, which is where raspberry bushes thrive.

FROZEN MANGO SLING

1 ½ oz (45 ml) Absolut Apeach

½ oz (15 ml) peach liqueur

½ oz (15 ml) lemon juice

½ oz (15 ml) simple syrup

1 diced mango

Crushed ice

Pour all the ingredients into a blender. Blend briefly at high speed until smooth. Start with a small amount of crushed ice and add more until you achieve the desired thickness. Serve in a highball glass and garnish with fresh mango.

Mango is the national fruit of India and Pakistan and is full of goodies including carotene and antioxidants, but it also contains urushiol, something it has in common Brazil nuts. Allergy sufferers should exercise some caution, at least when handling the peel.

BLACKBERRY BEAST

1 ½ oz (45 ml) absinth

½ oz (15 ml) Crème de Mûre

1 oz (30 ml) cranberry juice

6 mint leaves

5 blackberries

2 tbsp blueberry puree

1 tsp demerara sugar

Champagne

Muddle the blackberries, mint leaves and sugar in a shaker. Fill up with a scoop of crushed ice and add absinth, Crème de Mûre, puree and cranberry juice. Shake well. Strain into a highball glass and fill up with more crushed ice. Top with champagne and stir gently. Garnish with mixed berries.

Judging by the long list of ingredients, this mixture may appear slightly mad. And what about the absinth? Doesn't it drive you insane? No, research shows that the old recipe only contained harmless amounts of the toxin, which suggests that the monstrous effects were due to nothing but sheer drunkenness. This cocktail is indeed a bit of a beast, but definitely worth the trouble!

FROZEN PEACH DAIQUIRI

2 oz (60 ml) light rum

1 ½ oz (45 ml) peach puree

1 oz (30 ml) lime juice

½ oz (15 ml) simple syrup

Crushed ice

Pour all the ingredients into a blender. Blend briefly at high speed until smooth. Start with a small amount of crushed ice and add more until you achieve the desired thickness. Serve in a margarita glass.

TIP! For a more intense peach flavour, replace the simple syrup with peach juice.

Christopher Columbus brought the first sugar canes from Asia to Cuba in the 15th century, which is good for us, because it's impossible to produce rum without sugar.

BLOODY MARY

2 oz (60 ml) vodka

1 dash Worcestershire sauce

¼ tsp salt

¼ tsp pepper

½ oz (15 ml) lemon juice

2 dashes Tabasco

Tomato juice

Celery stick for garnish

Pour the first six ingredients into an ice-filled highball glass. Fill up with tomato juice and stir. Garnish with a celery stick.

Best known as the world's number one hangover cure – perhaps due to its saltiness. Many believe that this cocktail was named after Mary I, the bloodthirsty queen of England who was known for her many executions. A more likely story involves Pete Petiot, bartender at Harry's New York Bar in Paris and a Mary Pickford fan. Mary Pickford was a silent movie star known as 'the whole world's little sweetheart'. 'Bloody' would then refer to the drink's colour.

THAI MOJITO

2 oz (60 ml) Havana Club Añejo Reserva

½ lime

1 tsp demerara sugar

½ oz (15 ml) ginger juice

6 coriander leaves

1 chilli for garnish

Muddle the lime, coriander, sugar
and half of the chilli in a tumbler.
Fill up the glass with crushed ice,
add rum and stir. Serve with a straw
and garnish with chilli and coriander
leaves.

Fresh grated ginger is used in much the same way as dried ginger, but it is juicier and crisper.
Ginger was first brought to Northern Europe by the Romans, and it was one of the most popular
spices of the Middle Ages.

SANGRIA

Serves 10–15

2 bottles sweet Spanish red wine

4 oz (120 ml) Cointreau

3 oz (90 ml) brandy

3 oz (90 ml) orange juice

2 oz (60 ml) lemon juice

2 oz (60 ml) lime juice

8 oz (240 ml) simple syrup

Orange slices

Lemon slices

Lime slices

Grapes

Pour all the liquid ingredients into a large bowl (or two pitchers) and give everything a good stir. Add a pint of ice cubes and the fruit.

TIP! Sangria is a type of Spanish punch to which all sorts of fruits and berries can be added. Try replacing the oranges with peaches, and why not add a few cups of iced black tea? Instead of juices, you can use various soft drinks, and you can vary the strength and intensity by increasing or decreasing the amount of brandy. Brandy can also be excluded altogether or replaced with vodka.

The word Sangria comes from *sangre,* the Spanish word for blood, probably because of the blood-red colour of this popular party punch. It is the perfect drink for a summer social . It is deliciously refreshing, but be careful – it is a lot stronger than the sweet taste leads you to believe ...

STRAWBERRY COLADA

1 ½ oz (45 ml) white rum

½ oz (15 ml) strawberry liqueur

½ oz (45 ml) thick coconut milk

2 oz (60 ml) pineapple juice

½ oz (15 ml) double cream

4 strawberries + 1 for garnish

Crushed ice

Pour the ingredients into a blender. Blend briefly at high speed until smooth. Pour into an exotic hurricane glass and garnish with fresh strawberries.

In general, women have more taste buds on their tongues than men, which normally makes them more sensitive to strong and intense flavours. The difference can be enormous –one person can have 11 taste buds per square centimetre and someone else 1,100! There are, of course, individual differences, but this could be a reason why women are often prone to liking sweet and fruity 'girly drinks' such as this ...

STRAWBERRY DAIQUIRI

2 oz (60 ml) light rum

4–6 strawberries

1 oz (30 ml) lime juice

½ oz (15 ml) simple syrup

Crushed ice

Pour all the ingredients into a blender. Blend briefly at high speed until smooth. Start with a small amount of crushed ice and add more until you achieve the desired thickness. Serve in a margarita glass and garnish with fresh strawberries.

Almost as well-known as the original, Frozen Strawberry Daiquiri is simply a must in the summer. It's bound to seduce just about anyone ...

ACKNOWLEDGMENTS

I would like to thank my dear husband and agent, **Stefan Lindström**, who always believes in me and my crazy ideas. I appreciate our long and uplifting discussions that have brought me new ideas and fresh inspiration. I also want to thank you for tasting and judging every recipe found in this book. I would also like to thank my dear brother, **Alan Maranik**, for the beautiful design – working with you is always an inspiration, and my dear sister, **Adriana Maranik**, for her help with adapting the translated text to the layout.

I would also like to thank **Sara Hallström** who did the research – you are a gem! My editor, **Rebecka Wolff** for her fantastic input and **Katarina Trodden** for translating the book into English. Thank you **Roland Glukhov**, who helped me during photo sessions and post-processing, and many thanks to **Tony Greenwood** and **Hannah Jarvis Howard** at Massolit, London, and the **Turnaround** sales team. And finally, I would like to thank the **Marriott Marbella Beach Resort** and the **Key West Marriott Beachside Hotel** for being such inspirational and wonderful places for a writer.

Eliq Maranik

FROM THE SAME PUBLISHER

ELIQ MARANIK

THE COCKTAIL BOOK

- 250 RECIPES
- COCKTAIL HISTORY
- TRIVIA

THE COCKTAIL BOOK

Fancy a cocktail party? Now you have the chance to mix all your favourite drinks at home!

Here you will find more than 250 different cocktail recipes. The selection of cocktails is intended as an inspiration for the novice as well as the more experienced home bartender. The cocktails vary in number of ingredients and complexity of preparation, but they have one thing in common – they're delicious!

The Cocktail Book includes a section on glass types and equipment and advices you on which spirits, liqueurs and juices to use. You will also find a thorough guide to all the technical terms and expressions used in bartending, a comprehensive history of alcoholic beverages and a fascinating account of the manufacturing of spirits. Each drink recipe is accompanied by trivia and fun facts, often relating to the historical people and myths surrounding the drinks. There simply can be no cocktail book without Mr Hemingway!

The book is aimed towards the wide population of cocktail lovers. It contains all the old classics, but also plenty of trendy novelties. You will find the old familiar cocktails in many new guises, often with an international, exciting flavour.

In short, this a complete collection of cocktails ideal for surprising your friends on a Saturday night, but also for boosting your own cocktail skills and knowledge!

ISBN 978-1-908233-05-9

FROM THE SAME PUBLISHER

WHISKY & FOOD

Jan Groth is Global Scotch Brand Ambassador for the largest group of whisky producers in the world. He feels privileged to be able to teach people everything they need to know about whisky, learn from the best in the business and discuss food and whisky with chefs and celebrities.

In this book, Jan Groth describes his own and other people's favourite whiskies. It is a cookery book in disguise, in which foods and flavours are communicated through anecdotes and travel accounts in a most delicious way. It also includes useful tips on how whisky and food work together as well as a multitude of mouth watering whisky-inspired recipes by professional chefs.

This book is full of great pictures by Arne Adler of equally great food photographed in scenic inland and seaside locations across Scotland. Inspiring recipes and top of the line whiskies such as Talisker, Caol Ila and Ardbeg contribute to the pleasures of combining food and whisky, turning us all into whisky ambassadors. Slainté Maith! Dinner is served.

ISBN 978-1-908233-04-2

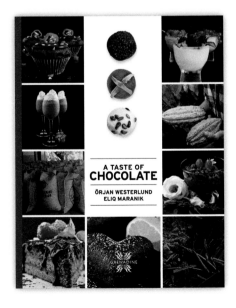

A TASTE OF CHOCOLATE

There is something about chocolate – this sinfully delicious, infinitely beloved treat symbolising pleasure and passion for the eye as well as the palate. We now bring you this pleasure in book form – a book for the real chocoholic!

In *A Taste of Chocolate*, you will find everything you have ever wanted to know about this immensely popular delight: history, manufacture, trivia and much more. In addition, the book contains a collection of 36 heavenly tempting chocolate recipes illustrated with seductive photographs. You will be sure to find your new favourite recipes, not only of classics such as chocolate truffles and chocolate fondant, but also innovative creations such as spicy chilli-chocolate muffins and espresso mousse, or how about a yummy Kahlúa brownie?

ISBN 978-1-908233-08-0